THE *Dying Art* OF EMAIL ETIQUETTE

Table of Contents

Forward 5
Preface 7
Chapter 1: The Dying Art. 11
Chapter 2: The Hierarchy. 19
Chapter 3: The Opening Salutation. 27
Chapter 4: The Closing Salutation 35
Chapter 5: The Signature 37
Chapter 6: The People. 65
Chapter 7: The Subject 75
Chapter 8: The Message. 91
Chapter 9: The Tone 109
Chapter 10: The Reply 137
Chapter 11: Final Remarks 143

Introduction

Forward

A journey through the history and origin of written communication from the times where there was no other way to communicate. Outlining the skill, thought and grandiose storytelling in order to make clear why writing an email can and should be much more than just a brain dump was a fabulous way of writing this book. Jared took the time to tell the stories and explain the impact of those stories on the recipient.

This book changed the way I write emails forever. If you want to stick out as someone who actually cares about the little things with massive impact, this is your book.

Steven Kuhn

Quality of Life Enterprises

Vetpreneur Tribe

Co-Author of "Unleash Your Humble Alpha"

Preface

Before we dive into the content, there are some things that need to be said first. I do not claim to be an email expert. Furthermore, I've never studied any type of etiquette regarding communication methods or tools. Everything delivered here is a direct result of my observations and experiences.

This book is not designed to be utilized for email marketing. The purpose of this book is specifically written for human-to-human emails. So, we're looking at the email communication within an organization, and with the organization's customers. Simply put, the traditional workplace.

The electronic mail (e-mail, or email) started taking over the world in the 1990s. I've used email for the majority of my life, and yet no one has ever trained or taught me how to utilize it properly. It's something that we all have self-taught ourselves. At the very least, I'd expect to have received a lesson in how to write an email during my college writing courses. Yet, there were no email related writing made available.

It was during the 90s that companies like Yahoo and American On-Line (AOL) began taking over the world. This is about the time when chat rooms were created that would allow users with a valid email account to chat in a group on any desired topic. It was here that the world first began to experience short-handed languages.

These short-hand languages were words that were assembled to represent a specific message. These messages were subsequently turned into acronyms to expedite a response. These acronyms generally followed the first character of the words being utilized, which made it easier to remember. Some of the most popular acronyms during these days were ASL, TTFN and BRB.

ASL referred to "age/sex/location" and emerged as a quick way for people to get a baseline of information about the people they were talking with. Which was also utilized heavily in the flirting/sexual/cyber chatrooms as well.

TTFN was what many ladies would use to sign off with, stating "ta ta for now" which was a goodbye that surged in the 90s. It's hard to know exactly where this came from, but it was used quite frequently in Disney's Winnie the Pooh movie and television appearance by Tigger (the lovable tiger).

BRB stands for "be right back". This was used when you had to step away from your computer for any number of reasons. Anything like getting a drink, using the bathroom, heading down the street to the store, etc. was all covered under BRB.

So, why does any of this matter?

PREFACE

During the world of chat rooms, people became accustomed to typing out exactly what they thought without consideration of others. This was the first time in the world, that you could be anyone you wanted to be ONLINE. You could be who you want, and you could say what you want. All without worrying about any potential ramifications. Why is that? Because your screen name could be anything you wanted it to be, no one has seen your face, and therefore they can't identify who you are.

Again, this is long before the advanced tracking technology that we have today in 2020. During those days, police had to go undercover in these chat rooms, or even in private chatting in the hopes that you would reveal who you really are and what your location is.

Almost simultaneously, at the same pace that email and chat rooms were growing, text messaging was invented and excelling along the same path.

When the text message was first released, the world experienced a new way to communicate with other people. Yes, we had emails and chat rooms, but those required the use of a computer. This was the first typed out communication that didn't require a computer.

For those who may not remember, the numbered keypad was the only way to write out a text message. Naturally, when this started, we all utilized the keypad to write out a message in the exact manner as we spoke. Therefore, all messages were following somewhat of a proper grammar structure.

As time progressed, along with the chat rooms, another version of short-handed communication emerged. With the growing slang used in the 90s, this instantly was adopted into text messaging talk. The reason for this is not only because it was popular, but also because it was easier to get the message out.

Think of today's short-hand messaging. LOL is probably the most popular acronym on the internet. If you're not familiar with it, LOL stands for "Laugh Out Loud". It's common way in today's society to basically state that something was funny. On an old-school numbered keypad, it would take significantly longer to type out twenty plus letters as it is to type three letters.

Due to the desire to be more efficient (in other words being primarily too lazy to push 100 buttons to say something simple) in getting the message across, many people embraced these short-hand acronyms.

It's because of this, and the fact that chat rooms were unregulated during this time, was the start of the communication declining curve, as we'll call it.

CHAPTER 1

The Dying Art

Email is the modern-day letter writing. In order to better understand the concepts of an email, we must first recognize their origins in letter writing. I understand that there are many people in this world that have never experienced this, but it's important to understand the beginnings.

So, how would you write a letter?

First, let's start with personal letters. Obviously, you'll need to find a piece of paper, preferably lined, and you grab a pen or pencil. Then, at the top of the letter you typically begin with a greeting or salutation. Long ago, society was generally always formal in a letter, and so we'll use that here.

In a personal letter, you would start with "Dear" and follow it by either the first name, or you would use their title (Mr./Mrs./Ms./Dr./etc.) followed by their last name.

Examples:

Dear John
Dear Mr. Smith
Dear Mrs. Smith
Dear Ms. Smith
Dear Dr. Smith

This will give us an opening that invites the reader into reading more of the letter. You've utilized their name in the appropriate context and opened by being polite and cordial to the reader. The actual level of formality that is utilized is based on your relationship with the person. Long ago, you only used first names of family members that were on your level or lower.

For example, you would use the name of your spouse, siblings or children, but would never do that with your parents. For them, you'd still say father or mother.

From there we embark on a journey to write the body of the letter. While some can be only a few sentences, most are about one page, and in uncertain times of war or separation from loved ones, it's generally much longer. Spanning from live with love, to the destruction of war, and everything in between.

Regardless of what is being said in the letter, there are similarities in these letters. There is generally a logical flow to what is being written, and it almost always tells a story of some kind. During letter writing days, the logical flow was generally telling a series of events in chronological order.

During these times, when writing a letter, you might have to start over several times. Think about writing in pen on actual paper. You can't erase the pen marks, and so if you were to make a mistake, you'd basically be wasting that paper and would have to start over. It's because of this that people would put quite a lot of thought into writing each sentence of a letter before they actually wrote it down.

This was generally done to conserve paper or ink. The world was frugal like that during those days, which is a direct result from hard times like the Great Depression.

But there is something more deeper happening here outside what is being said in these letters. It's the tone that is being used in the letter. When you were away in a war, your loved one had to convey her love for you in these letters. Not only by simply stating "I love you" but through the tone used throughout the letter itself.

And finally, when the body of the letter is finished, you'll write out another salutation to effectively end the letter. For loved ones, you would generally write "love", "with love" or something of that nature. Then below it you would sign the letter with your name. This gave the letter that added personal feeling of authenticity, so whoever was reading the letter would know it was really you.

Why does any of this matter?

I've used email for most of my life in personal communication, which is about thirty years. In my career, I've been using email for about fifteen years now. Then in my entrepreneur path, I've been using email for about eight years. So, collectively across all avenues, that's over fifty years of experience using emails.

I don't doubt that they are millions of people out there who are in the exact same position as I am. The difference between me and the majority of them is how I perceive the usage of the email, how I relay information, and how I personally believe that the world needs more of when sending emails.

Over the years, I've seen a steady decline in how people communicate in their emails. We all know that letter writing is virtually dead, and for anyone still doing it, they are way ahead of the rest of the world. Why is this?

It's quite simple really. The whole world is only really focused on a few types of communication. These three types of communicating top the cake, and everything else has fallen to the wayside. They are the "post", the "comment", and the "message". This is how we communicate in today's society, but they aren't the only ways that we communicate, and many people tend to forget that.

The "post" refers to social media posting. When posting on social media, we, as a society, typically utilize the modern form of short-hand language. This includes by extension the excessive use of emojis, imagery and memes.

The "comment" refers to how we respond to a post. There are generally reaction buttons that display icons and emojis. Then, the actual wording of a comment utilizes the same principles of the post. We utilize short-hand language, emojis, imagery and memes quite excessively.

The "message" refers to text messaging and chatting options. For chatting, I'm specifically referring to any type of private messaging. It could be something broad like Google Hangouts, or something specific to a social media platform like Facebook Messenger. Nonetheless, this type of chatting is generally referred to as PM (private message) or DM (direct message). Even though this type of communication is more private than the rest, we still resort to utilizing the same techniques as the other avenues of communication. We use the short-hand language, emojis, imagery and memes.

When you look at these three "primary" types of communication for the mass population in society you'll notice some trends. Society tends to use the same techniques across all mediums, and in this case its' the short-hand language, emojis, imagery and memes. These methods of communicating are excessively utilized in all of these "primary" outlets.

If you've never written a letter, or its' been awhile, you might be asking yourself "Why does that matter?" It's because the world has an outlet to speak freely without any ramifications, and the fact that this new form of communicating is excessively utilized that people will forget how to properly utilize the language.

My daughter, who is in elementary school, came home one day saying "OMG" and "cra-cra". For those who are unfamiliar with this lingo, "OMG" stands for "Oh My God" (or "Oh My Gosh") and "cra-cra" stands for "crazy".

Almost instantly, I was furious with her for talking like this. I proceeded to tell her (angrily, of course) that I've never spoke to her like that, and she will never talk in our house like that either. I told her to use English properly, and to never use that crap she picks up from school and her friends.

Many people reading this might think that I would be overreacting, and they might be right. But for sake of argument, let me put some context into it.

My daughter is half-Japanese, and English wasn't her first language. She grew up speaking Japanese and didn't actually start speaking English until about four or five years old when she started pre-school here in America.

Naturally, my wife and I have many talks with our children about using the language properly. My wife talks to her about using Japanese properly, and I do the same with English. We do this because she's maintaining the knowledge of two languages, and we remind her about the proper usage of words, grammar and context. It's important to my wife and I that our children speak both English and Japanese so that our children can communicate with both of our families without needing a translator.

Putting all of that aside though, children are highly impressionable. They learn things at a young age, which could include bad language and bad behavior, and it sticks with them for decades later. On the other side of the coin, children could learn good behavior and proper language, which would not only stick with them, but also help them excel far beyond their peers.

This is the true reasoning behind my comments. I'd never taught my daughter to use any "text talk" as I call it, and I was severely shocked when I learned of this. Yes, I do recognize that my reaction could have been handled better, but I do not shy away from or regret what I said to her.

You might, yet again, be thinking "why does this matter?". I tell you all of this because our communication foundation is broken. We, as a society, need to get "back to basics", and need to rebuild the foundation of our language. Realistically, its' not that hard to fix. Every organization leader, university president, or business owner could take a simple step to reinforce the use of proper language. You could mandate it. Write a policy mandating the proper use of languages and monitor to eradicate this "text talk" within your organizations.

I've done just this within my own organization. Naturally, I'm running a small shop, and all "employees" are subcontractors on an "as needed" basis right now. Yet, I do mandate the use of proper English and will still put them in check when they try to use "text talk" or any form or short-hand language. The only thing I allow is the use of "LOL" and a few emojis, and they are only allowed in messaging mediums.

This too probably sounds "cra-cra" (or crazy) I'm sure. But by doing this, I'm effectively forcing everyone that works with me to actually write out everything. When you write out everything, over time, you're writing skills will naturally increase. Your keyboarding skills increase, and your level of knowledge about the language increases.

For people who are really bad, I'll even recommend Grammarly, which is a free piece of software that will help you re-write your content. I would gladly accept this over a text message styled email that uses an excessive amount of emojis.

Lastly, when you write a proper email, it will make you look better. Since they are so many people in the world who can't write up a proper email, just following the basics alone will make you look more professional and a better person all around. So, it can't hurt, right?

I urge everyone reading this to fully adopt all principles that are presented in this book. I've used all of them in my career and my business. You will have to actively be contentious about using these principles. You will need to monitor what you do. For some, that find it harder to follow, I'd even recommend that you build an email checklist.

Regardless of how intense you need to monitor your email usage; it won't make a difference unless you actively want to improve yourself. So, if you don't care about getting better, then just stop reading now, because its' going to take work. Lots of it.

It takes a lot of energy to make sure you are actively using these methods and principles in all of your email communication. Even to this day, and yes even after writing this book, I still have to run through my mental checklist before sending an email.

Moving forward, everything that we discuss will be derived from business and the workplace. It's important to understand how these concepts are applied in the workplace, so that we can recognize them in our personal communication as well.

CHAPTER 2

The Hierarchy

Understanding the hierarchy is critical to your email writing. Knowing who is on your team is a given, including your supervisor, but knowing who all of the important people in your organization are is significantly more powerful.

In the military, we are, in many cases, required to know the entire hierarchy, all the way to the top of the organization and beyond. Which in the military, it's from where you are all the way up to the "Commander in Chief", or the President of the United Stated of America. We call this the "chain of command".

When you know who is in your chain, you can then ensure that your emails are addressed appropriately. You definitely can't send out emails to your bosses' boss that says, "what's up guy"? That's how you get fired. So, understanding your chain is crucial to your overall email success.

The Golden Rule says "Tread others the way you want to be treated".

How do you want to be treated in the workplace? Naturally, you'd want to be treated with respect, and so that's exactly what we are going to deliver. We give our respect, under the guise of goodwill, so that we in turn get back respect.

Here is an example of what a department may look like.

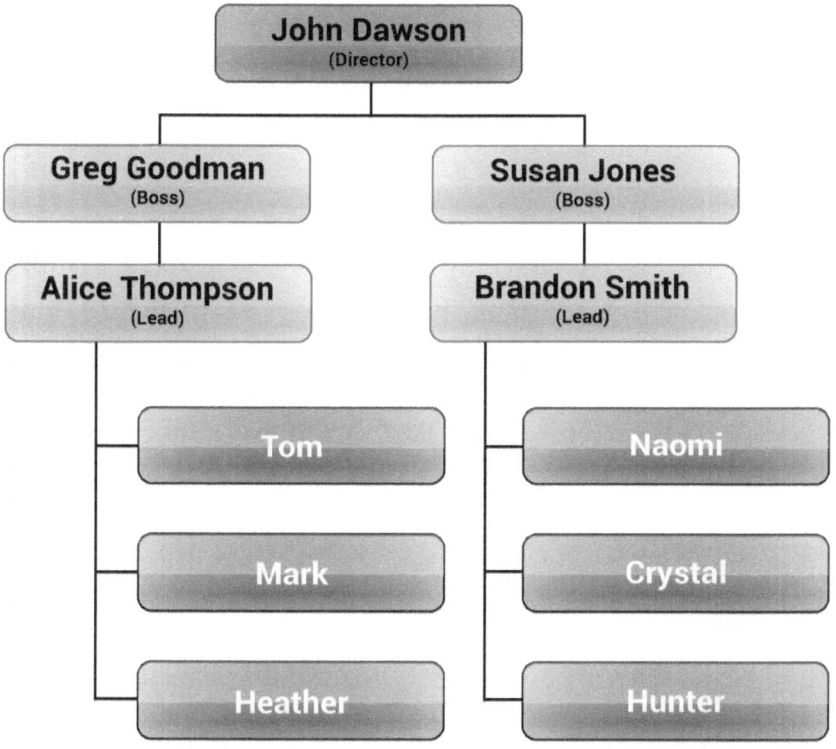

You'll notice right away that this organizational chart has last names for everyone that has some type of authority. This is by design for our example.

Let's say that you're Mark, and your team members are Tom and Heather. You will most definitely be working closely with these two and will undoubtably be on a first name basis with them. That's how almost every organization in the world will work. Based on this example, these people are your peers. Of course, there can be more layers of complexity here. Each of those layers need to be addressed appropriately, but for the sake of simplicity, here is our organization.

A little bit about me, I grew up in the south. It has been deeply ingrained into me to show respect to my elders. If I ever wasn't, then I'd be expecting my grandmother to show up and beat my ass. So, anyone who looks older than me, I will naturally show them respect. This comes with a certain level of politeness, by calling my elders "sir" or "ma'am".

To dive deeper, I was also in the Marine Corps. All officers were addressed as "sir" and "ma'am". Also, any civilian personnel that we worked with were also given the same respect. This is something that is deeply ingrained into every Marine, and we were always expected to communicate this way. I wouldn't know about every other branch, but I suspect it's very similar in this case.

So, it's safe to assume that I'll never stray away from this. I do have one caveat though, and this is something I picked up during my career. When I first started working with people that were significantly older than I, they were naturally addressed with "sir" and "ma'am". In many cases, I was told repeatedly to not call them that. Needless to say, I can't stop doing it. But I would attempt to concede by calling them by their first name. And it would "slip" if they asked me a question.

This is something I've never seen as a problem for myself, but others may view this differently. So, even today, I'll attempt to call my elders by their first name, but I can't control my politeness, so at some point in time, I'll call them "sir" or "ma'am". It's going to happen.

So, now when I'm told to not someone "sir" or "ma'am", I'll let them know upfront. I'll try, but it's not within my control. That's because it has been so deeply ingrained within me.

I say all of this to throw some light on the fact that you may have peers that are technically your elders, but it's generally okay to be more informal with them. For me, this has been the only time I've ever been informal with an elder.

Next, you have your Team Lead, and in our situation it's Alice Thompson. Depending on how your department is structured, you may or may not be on a first name basis with Alice. In some cases, you'll refer to her as Mrs. Thompson instead of just calling her Alice. I've always tried to find a happy medium in this. In short, I prefer to always be formal in emails.

I've tried to be friendly and informal in person, but for some reason, I will almost always pull back on the reigns in my emails. So, I'll talk to you and use your first name, but when it comes to "official correspondence" (basically, work related messages and emails), then I'll go back to basics and get formal once again.

Back In 2015, it was my first time being exposed to the civilian (non-military) team lead. The lady running my team, or the team I was on, came from a different background as me and for reasons unknown, we clicked fairly well. This could be because we were about the same age, or the fact that I had a gnarly beard like her husband. Regardless, almost instantly, I was communicating with her on an informal basis in all of our conversations.

We had a good work relationship, and even today, we stay in touch. But there is one thing I could never bring myself to do, and that's address her informally in my emails. It's like the southern hospitality and the Marine inside me are constantly on guard and won't let it happen.

At this point, you might be saying that I'm crazy, and you may be right. I probably have a screw loose somewhere. I actually don't dwell on what other people think about me. So, it doesn't really matter.

In the Marine Corps, my Military Occupational Specialty (MOS) was internally recognized as Supply Admin. Needless to say, I used a computer daily. I would write and send emails to my coworkers, leaders in my chain, and quite frequently, other organizations. In the military, everyone is addressed by their last name, and prefixing it would be your rank. So, I would've been called Lance Corporal (LCpl) Ledbetter when LCpl was my rank.

When writing out emails to any other Marines, I'd always utilized the proper addressing. So, if I was sending an email to LCpl Smith, then that's exactly how I would address them; as LCpl Smith. This is what I would use every single time.

When that is translated, for non-Marines, that would naturally be Mr. Smith, or Mrs./Ms. Smith. So, what I'm saying is that my email game is strong. If I could get paid based on the effectiveness of my emails, I'd be a billionaire by now. And as we've stated before, that effectiveness is based on initially how you address people.

This isn't the case for every situation. For the past couple of years now, I've noticed that I have a problem with my current role. For a while, during the interim on a Team Lead's pending retirement, I had three Team Leads. That's right, for several months, I had three Team Leads. The retirement has since gone through, and I'm down to two, but the department actually wants two Team Leads.

I take several issues with my current employer. There are problems with the agency's culture, organizational structure, data, and finally the people. It's by far the worst place I've ever worked, and that's saying a lot for me. Honestly, I could spend my whole life fixing this place and never make a dent. So, when it comes to my Team Leads, I've got no patience with them. They actually buy into the culture, in most cases, and don't really care about the data problems. As long as the customer is happy, and the hellfire doesn't come down on them, they are happy.

Naturally, I personally take issue with this. I've prided my career on being the best, doing everything right, and always following procedures. But now I'm faced with something new because I have never not been formal in addressing my Team Lead. And now, my views on the organization, my department and the people are affecting how I address my Team Leads. I think this is called growth, but I'm not sure. It's only happening with Team Leads and no one else. So, maybe it's just them. Only time will tell.

I tell you this only under the guise of transparency. I'm not perfect, and none of us are. Yes, I'm writing this book out of a perceived need, but even I struggle with this concept and have to actively pursue it. Otherwise, I'll become the thing I despise most; being mediocre.

Moving on from the Team Lead, you've got your supervisor. Much like the officer's in the Corps, I've never addressed a supervisor informally in an email. The same goes for anyone above my supervisor in my chain. I'd go as far to say that it never will happen for me, and even more so for supervisors that I dislike.

Much like letter writing, how you address a person is dependent on your relationship with them. In the workplace this is really simple. Anyone who is your direct peer or co-worker and below, you can and should address them by their first name. In fact, this is exactly what I do, and I do this regardless of their age.

The first level above you is based on you. So, shift managers or team leads, it's going to be up to you. Again, I'd be typically formal here, but I'm currently in a weird spot.

For your supervisor, and anyone at or above the same level as your supervisor, your only option is to be formal. In fact, there are many times when you need to email someone that you don't know, or from another department. It's these instances that I'm also extremely formal. My formality in these situations is based on general politeness and perception. If people perceive you to be polite, then they perceive the organization to be polite. So, no one is losing ground over me.

Lastly comes the discussion of addressing a person in multiple instances. In the opening greeting of my email, it's typical for me to utilize "Sir" and "Ma'am". When the email is addressed to one person it's easy for them to recognize who you're talking about. So, there is no need to call their name.

Then, if I need to identify them in the body, this is where I'll use Mr./Mrs. and their last name. The only time that I deviate from this, and use their name in the greeting, is when the email has many people on it, or it is addressed to multiple people.

When I say, "many people", I'm talking about those emails that start as a couple of people and build to include forty people from twelve departments. When an agency doesn't fully understand how to embrace the technology, this stuff will happen all the time.

In fact, this happens in my current role all the time. So, we identify who we are talking to in order to prevent confusion for the masses. It's really a preventative measure. All too many times, I've seen people asking, "is this for me?" in a mass email to forty or more people. This just goes to boast your incompetence, and I'll never stand up for these people.

If you are unsure if the email is for you (ON A MASS EMAIL), then pick up the phone, call the sender and ask them straight out. That way you don't look like an idiot in front of your boss, his boss and their boss.

CHAPTER 3

The Opening Salutation

The opening salutation, once the email is opened, is the first thing in the email body that people will read. Over the years, I've seen a handful of salutations, which include the non-existent ones.

An official business letter would typically start off with the salutation of "Dear", "Greetings" or even "To Whom It May Concern". All of which are utilized based on the situation and tone of the letter. This traditional use of letter greetings has virtually died over the years with the emergence of email.

There are still situations outside the workplace where the aforementioned greetings are still utilized. For, example, if you were following up with a potential employer, you could utilize "To Whom It May Concern" and do well with it.

In today's society, even more so in the tech industry, it's highly common to be more informal. This informal line of communication is based on getting more interpersonal with the customers but also to break barriers and cut through to the customer.

Being informal has it's place. These types of greetings are generally using "Hi", "Hello", "Hey" or just the person's name. While this may do well with communicating with customers in the tech space, it's important to realize that this isn't always the best course of action. Maybe, as the next generation comes to power, that could change quite significantly, but today that isn't the case.

The problem with using an informal greeting like this is that you lose the professionalism in your communications. In the Marine Corps, you are trained early on to maintain your professionalism in all your encounters. This high level of professionalism is basically mandated in all that you do. It's because of this that I'll likely never change my approach in my own email writing.

One of the most common ways to achieve professionalism is by giving the "greeting of the day". For those of you who don't know what I'm talking about, the greeting of the day is referred to the greeting that is based on the time of day. The time of day would be either morning, afternoon or evening. Therefore, the greeting of the day would be "Good Morning", "Good Afternoon" or "Good Evening".

This greeting is then followed by a formal honorific and name. The honorific is the title based on status, position or billet. So, for most people that would be "Mr.", "Mrs." or "Ms.". For doctors you would use "Dr.", or even high-level government officials you might refer to them as "Honorable Mr.", "Honorable Mrs.", etc.

These formal opening salutations are exactly what I utilize in virtually every email that I write; regardless of the recipient. That's one of the many qualities that I've picked up from the Corps, but I'm not upset about this habit.

I couldn't even begin to quantify how many emails that I've seen that didn't utilize the greeting of the day. It's sad to say, that it's almost none. In almost every email that I've ever received, I've never seen the greeting of the day. It's quite astounding, and almost like I've found a secret that no one has ever heard of.

During my time in the Marine Corps, I've seen a few types of greetings that always involved my last name. For anyone who has ever served in the military/police, this will not be a surprise. My subordinates, and sometimes my peers or superiors, would open up with "Cpl Ledbetter". Then, you'd have some peers and superiors that might just call me "Ledbetter".

As my career took me out of the Corps, I became "Mr. Ledbetter", or simply "Jared". Then there are always those who will start off their emails as "Hello Jared", "Hi Jared" or "Hey Jared". And yet, fourteen years of my career is completed, and I still don't see anyone else utilizing the greeting of the day.

Another trend that has popped up in recent years, is to not use a greeting at all. Just jump right into the email without saying anything. Which is the furthest down the drain you can go. What's worse, is that I see this lack of greeting to come from my elders more than not. People who are fifty years old, or older, are more prone to not utilize a greeting at all.

I've actually never recalled receiving an email with the same level of greeting professionalism that I've delivered. It's a sad, cruel world.

The opening salutation is the one moment that people have to make a decision on who you are as a person.

It's because of this that people believe that using the informal greeting is the best. Because it would relay that you are friendly or easy to talk to. In email marketing, and transactional emails, this can do well. But when you're looking at the workplace and communicating with a person, it's actually better to show that you are a true professional.

What do I mean by "true professional"?

Well, it's exactly as I stated before. Your opening salutation is your introduction to gaining a person's trust. You can choose to be friendly, or you can choose to be a professional, and I always choose professional.

Internally, we all judge people based on a first impression, regular communication and their actions. My first impression with a person, and subsequently, the regular communication is always on that professional level.

I will actually take that a step further and implement that into my email communication. I will naturally show respect to anyone that I'm working with throughout the course of doing business. But the respect that I have for you, personally, will depend on what I observe, and your email is included.

THE OPENING SALUTATION

I get a lot of emails on my business email accounts, and most of them are spam. I'm sure we get those emails, but I really get an excessive amount. I couldn't tell you how many people have emailed me to offer me the exact services that are listed on my website. It's atrocious, really.

Yet, the only emails that I will take the time to read are the ones who use a proper greeting. And since none of them use one, I never read too far into their email. I'll scan it to verify it's not something that needs to get moved to my inbox, but I don't digest any of it.

People in the digital marketing world always talk about getting through to the decision maker. Well, if the decision maker is a true professional, then they will expect you to be as well. I'm not saying that you've got to wear a three-piece suit while you type out your emails, but you need to relay that you are professional in a very short amount of time. That's why I've consistently utilized my opening salutation formula at every stage, and with every person.

When you drill this enough, it becomes engrained. In the Marines, we would call this "muscle memory". Which is something that your muscles remember, even if your brain doesn't. In the Corps, we'd generally focus this type of training for combat-related tasks, but it can really be applied anywhere.

My email opening salutation formula is simple. For people that I'm close with, or know personally, I'll remove the honorific. Otherwise, this is exactly what I use for every email, regardless of who the recipient is. Also, if I use "Sir" or "Ma'am", then I'll drop the name.

SECRET SAUCE

"Greeting of the Day" + "Honorific" + "Name" = Opening Salutation

Greeting of the Day:

Good Morning
Good Afternoon
Good Evening

Honorific:

Mr.
Mrs.
Ms.
Dr.
Sgt (Sergeant, or use other military ranks)
Sir
Ma'am

Name:

John
Smith

This is really that simple. You deliver on a high level of professionalism at the beginning of your communication with someone, and you never let your guard down.

It sounds like it's a relentless barrage of crap that you have to remember. If you've never written an email like this, then it could easily seem that way, but in reality, you have to practice writing your emails this way. You need to build that muscle memory in your fingers until it becomes natural for you every time.

Once you get there, you're golden.

CHAPTER 4

The Closing Salutation

The closing salutation is similar to the opening salutation, but instead of opening the conversation, you're closing it and showing that you are done saying what you needed to say.

Think to a time when you'd write a letter, or give a card, to a loved one. At the very end of the letter, you would normally write something along the lines of "With Love" or "Love", and then sign the card. That is exactly what we are talking about here.

The closing salutation will need to be combined with a signature for the full effect, but they need to be recognized separately.

Just like the opening salutation, there are several formal and informal options to utilize in your closing salutation. The most common three that I've seen over the years are below. These have become so common, that I'd be surprised if we ever make a full swing back into proper salutations.

FAIL 1:

R/S,
Jared

FAIL 2:

V/R,
Jared

FAIL 3:

Jared

In the workplace setting, there are several closing salutations that are professional enough to use in your emails. "Sincerely" and "Respectfully" are the two best words to use in my opinion. Long ago, I used to use "Very Respectfully", and I've since transitioned to "Respectfully Sent".

There are a few others that can do well, but I don't use them. They are listed below.

Regards
Warm Regards
Best Regards
Kind Regards
All the Best

If you've been paying attention here, you'll notice the trend setting in. It's generally a combination of a small word and a big word that do the best in the reader's mind.

CHAPTER 5

The Signature

In letters, you end the letter with a signature. In emails, you end the email with a "signature". A signature consists of your pertinent contact information and organizational information that is deemed relevant.

Just like anything else, there is a right and a wrong way to do this. I've developed the structure of my signature over the course of years. It's important to note that there is a couple of schools of thought on the email signature.

When sending an email, there is a "plain text" option, and an "HTML" option. If you've ever played with this, then you may already know what I'm talking about. If not, I'll break it down for you.

Plain text is simply that; plain text. No colors, images or anything fancy in your email. Hypertext Markup Language (HTML) is the code language that is used to structure content in a website. It's been expanded to include emails as well. The

HTML version of an email allows you to use images, background colors, font colors, pictures on left and text on right, etc. HTML emails can handle quite a bit of fancy voodoo.

So, let's translate that into the schools of thought. There are many people out there, who will utilize an HTML signature for their email. Which includes pictures, boxes, fancy fonts, etc. While this can be highly effective, especially if you're in the creative space, I don't believe that it's for everyone.

I've personally taken the stance that we should be using as much plain text in our email signature as possible. When I first started using emails in the Marines, we only had the plain text option. It wasn't until about ten years later where the HTML was even an option.

If you've ever looked at an email from people that you don't know, you'll notice that all of the images have been removed for security reasons. You have to manually click a button to display the images and format the email as it was originally designed.

It's because I don't use an HTML-styled signature that I don't have to worry about any security issues removing my email signature. I've got friends in the digital space, while running my own digital agency, where every email that I get from them I'll have to manually select to show the images. Every time.

If a recipient of my emails doesn't click on the show all button, then they will still be able to see my email signature without having to potentially subject themselves to a virus. That's the reason why images and other content is not displayed.

It's because you can embed malicious content within images or links, etc.

My email structure is quite simple, for me at least, but it's highly structured and easy to use.

- Closing Remarks
- Closing Salutation
- Name
- Title
- Department
- Organization
- Email
- Work Phone
- Mobile Phone
- Website
- Quote
- Organization Legal

Closing Remarks

Early on in my career, I discovered that I was writing the same type of content as the last sentence in my email. This would be a final statement that referenced if the recipient had and questions to contact me. I recall typing this sentence out over and over again in every email.

It wasn't long before that was adapted and input into my email signature.

"If you have any questions, or concerns, please don't hesitate to ask."

It's quite simple really, but it's been highly effective over the years. It shows that I'm open to discussion on the topic in the email, and that I'm available to answer your questions as they arise.

Being open and available to a customer, or another department in your organization is one of the most important things that an organization can do. Communication is key, and you must communicate effectively with the people that you are working with.

I couldn't even begin to describe the problems that I've encountered, that could've been prevented if department "A" would've spoken to department "B" beforehand. Not only is this a common courtesy thing, its' also a preventative measure to ensure that your new software feature doesn't screw up everyone else involved.

So, it's important to be open and available. This portrays just that.

Of course, you could easily find something else that might fit your brand, or your organization a little better. You might even find a "creative" or more friendly way to relay this message, but I've always found that simple and direct has been more effective than cute and fluffy.

Closing Salutation

In the last chapter, we went over the closing salutation. The closing salutation that I use is "Respectfully Sent"

Name

When you are adding your name to the signature, it's important to know your audience. In my experience, during my time in the Corps, other Marines would follow the same structure as me. Since getting out of the Corps, it seems like no one else has ever heard of this structure.

If the organization that you work for is branded as "creative" or "playful", then it likely won't matter if you follow this structure or not. But the majority of people out there will be working for organizations that have a more serious tone.

It's because of this tone that I've always taken a very simple stance; to stary professional. As you can probably guess by now, that's easy to do. My name is always displayed in the exact same manner for every position that I've ever held.

That structure looks like this:

Honorific + Last Name + Comma + First Name + Middle Initial

So, for me that would look like this:

Mr. Ledbetter, Jared M.

I use this exact setup for all of my work emails throughout my career, for my small business, and for my personal emails.

Title or Billet / Title & Billet

For those of us that have been in the military, we'll understand this really quick. For everyone else, you might not understand what I'm talking about, so I'll explain it.

In the Corps, in all of the places that I worked, there were only a few titles that we had in our "shop" (or workplace). The short-hand title for my position was "Supply Admin Clerk", but we mostly just called it "Supply Admin". We also had warehouseman, whose short-hand title was "Supply Warehouse Clerk", which we just called them "Supply Warehouseman". We also had numbered designations for these job titles, which were also used quite frequently.

There are several definitions of billets, but I'll refer to a billet in the workplace. In the administrative (admin) side of Supply, we had several positions within that were referred to as billets. If my position was to use data-entry to order and receipt for parts, that was my billet. If my position was to manage the inventory for our large items, then that was my billet.

In the rest of the world, you could have a team where everyone was hired under the same title. This is generally how Human Resources (HR) will keep track of personnel, hire personnel based on the position description, and in many cases your salary/wages are set by this title as well.

But your title doesn't always give enough information. That's where the billet can help. Here is an example to shed some light on this.

Let's say that you work in in customer support for a call center at Apple. What does that look like on paper? Your title is likely something generic like "Customer Support Representative" (CSR) or "Customer Support Specialist".

Apple has many products, too many to go through, but let's narrow it down to four main categories.

- iPhone (phones)
- iPad (tablets)
- MacBook (laptops)
- iMac (desktop computers)

Say that you worked customer support for iMacs (desktop computers). Your billet could be something like "iMac CSR", or "iMac Support". Then you get moved to another department. Your primary title won't change, because you'll still be listed as a "Customer Service Representative", but you'll be working in a different department. Now, working in the iPad (tablet) department, your new billet is the "iPad CSR" or "iPad Support".

I've had a few titles over the years, but I've had many billets. For example, when I worked at Defense Logistics Agency (DLA), my first title was "General Supply Specialist", but my billet was a "Resolution Specialist". We had other team members who were also a "General Supply Specialist" but their billet was "IDOC Specialist".

So, we were both paid on the same pay scale, our level of responsibility was similar, and we fit into the organization at the same level. But we had completely different duties, roles, responsibilities.

So, using this billet designation in your emails will help people to better understand what you do, or specifically where you work. This will help them to know if you are the right person to talk to or not.

Department

The department that you work in could mean several things. In reality, there are many organizations that are too small to have established departments, but that doesn't mean that you aren't in a different department.

If your organization doesn't have defined departments, then you could designate one for yourself. For example, if you are working in a small digital agency, and you do graphic design for products, social media, website, etc. then you could simply be just the "Graphics" department. Whereas, if you just worked on social media graphics, then you could be in the "Social Media Graphics" department.

When there is an absence of defined departments, this allows you to get a little creative to name your own department. It's important to note that this could be frowned upon, depending on who you work for, but it's important enough to have a discussion about it with your employer.

In one sub-contracted role, I actually didn't have a title established. So, I had to actually request one. Which was the sole purpose of adding it to my email signature. Sometimes, you'll have to do this with your department as well.

In larger organizations, your department name will likely have a coded designation. If that's the case, you need to know what that is. Especially, if your organization references a department by said coded designation.

Your department is simple to add to your signature. When your organization does have a coded designation that is utilized frequently, then it's imperative that you include that code with your department.

That would look something like this:

Department Code + Department Title = Department

Let's say that your organization is a manufacturing plant called "Safe Plastik". The organization makes plastic bottles and containers for food and drinks, like yogurt and soda. You work in the Finance department, and your billet is to work with the Purchase Cards. Basically, a company credit card.

Your organization has given the finance area the designation of "P8" (P for plastics). Then the department breaks down into Accounting, Purchasing & Payments. So, the Finance department looks like this:

P8 – Finance
P81 – Accounting
P811 – Journal
P812 - Taxes
P82 – Purchasing
P821 – Purchase Requisitions
P822 – Contracts
P823 – Purchase Cards

P83 – Payments
P831 – Accounts Payable
P832 – Accounts Receivable

So, if you work for the purchase cards, your actual department would be "P823 Purchase Cards". At the same time, if these department designations are not utilized out in the open, and you don't reference your department with the code, then you can leave it out.

When you do leave it out, however, you've got to add more details to anyone will know where you work. You would take off that "P823" and update it. Here are several alternative examples below.

Purchase Cards, Purchasing, Finance
Purchase Cards, Finance
Purchase Cards, Purchasing
Finance, Purchasing, Purchase Cards
Finance, Purchase Cards
Purchasing, Purchase Cards

In a letter, when you write an address at the top, it's common practice to identify where you are in the organization from the top down. So, for this plastic company here, your letterhead would look like this:

Safe Plastik
Finance
Purchasing
Purchase Cards

In emails, I take the inverse approach myself. So, my email would look like this:

Purchase Cards
Purchasing
Finance
Safe Plastik

It's because of this that my department (without the code designation) would be similar to this inverse approach. From the list of non-coded departments, I'd personally use "Purchase Cards, Purchasing, Finance".

In reality, you can use anything you want here, but you need to ensure that people can see exactly where you work, and where you are at in the hierarchy of the organization.

Organization

When it comes to the organization that you work for there are a few things to consider. The first is the actual organization you work for, and the second is where does that organization fall into the hierarchy of the entire organization. What do I mean by that? Let me show you.

When I worked for Defense Logistics Agency (DLA), I didn't work at the DLA headquarters level. I actually worked for a sub-organization called Disposition Services, and I was at the headquarters level. There are also many people who work at a field site that is specific to a location.

Let's take that faux plastic company from before and break it out into multiple locations.

Safe Plastik – Charlotte, NC is where the headquarters is located at.

Safe Plastik – Atlanta, GA is where all plastic container production takes place.

Safe Plastik – Memphis, TN is where the warehouses are located that store all of this product that is shipped out based on client needs.

Let's say that the Atlanta location is a sub-organization called SP Production, and the Memphis location is a sub-organization called SP Logistics.

Your title is the Transportation Clerk (scheduling all of the trucks that come in and pick up product, and all of the trucks that drop off product). You're located in Memphis where the warehouses are.

Your organization could look like one of the following:

Safe Plastik, SP Logistics
SP Logistics, Safe Plastik

Both of these show that you're working in a sub-organization of Safe Plastik, and that is the most important part of identifying your organization. People need to know where you work, and what organization you work for. Providing detail down to this level will provide more information to the people you're working with.

Let's say that the SP Logistics sub-organization has multiple sub-organizations under it and you're located in the SP Transport sub-agency.

You can provide even more detail, and break it down further. Your organization could look like one of the following:

Safe Plastik, SP Logistics, SP Transport
Safe Plastik, SP Transport
SP Logistics, SP Transport
SP Transport, SP Logistics, Safe Plastik
SP Transport, SP Logistics
SP Transport, Safe Plastik

In my experience, I've never used more than two organization declarations. One is ideal, two adds more detail, but three or more just gets to be too much for people to digest. It also makes your email signature look really bloated, and we don't want to do that.

In the example above, I'd probably use "SP Transport, Safe Plastik". This will keep me in that two-organization range but also provide enough info to let everyone know that I work for SP Transport, and it's under the umbrella of Safe Plastik.

Email

The email section is really simple. In general, you want to use all lowercase letters and numbers. From an Information Technology (IT) / Software perspective, every email is saved in lowercase letters. The reason for this is simple. When you are inputting your email to login to a web-based software, by default everything is case sensitive.

This means if you use an uppercase character, then your login will fail. That's why IT and developers have resorted to always saving the email as lowercase. With this method, you'll never run across an issue with a user trying to login.

It's the same with writing your email address in the signature itself. There are instances where I would advise to not use a lowercase system, but those instances are rare.

In most of those rare cases, you're working for a company that has a weird looking website domain. Since this is the case, you'll want to add the website link to your signature, and it's here where you would want to use proper capitalization to show people what the domain is referencing.

Let's say my email is jared.ledbetter@safeplastik.com. For anyone who has seen the company name before, this is really simple for people to understand what the company name is within the domain. There will always be people who can't recognize this, so I'll elaborate in the website domain section.

In practice, I will always prefix the email address with the actual text "email". So, my email address for Safe Plastik would look like this.

✉ Email: jared.ledbetter@safeplastik.com

In recent years, I've started adding the email envelope icon to my signature. With that addition my email line would look like this:

✉ Email: jared.ledbetter@safeplastik.com

The purpose of the icon is to capture their attention really quick when scanning over my email signature. Depending on your organization's policies and software, you might not be able to add an icon like I've done here, but it's worth looking into.

Work Phone

It's safe to say that most people will have a phone number for their office or workplace. Just like the email address, this is really simple to include. Before adding the phone number to your signature, you need to know what your organization policy is.

There are many organizations out there that have internal phone numbers, and a main number for customers to call. You need to know what your limitations are on this front.

I personally, would include my office number regardless. Not because I'm a rebel, but because I want people to be able to contact me when they need to. Not sit through an automated phone system, and maybe get to me. I can't stand automated phone systems, and I'll never subject people to it if I can prevent it.

Another thing to note is how your phone system is structured. Many organizations have a single number to call into, and then have various extensions to reach specific people.

If I ever had to implement extensions, I'd work in a bridged approach, where the last four of your number is your extension.

So, people could call you directly, or go through the extension system.

Like the email address, I've also started adding icons to my phone number signature line. Here are a couple of examples of what my phone line would look like.

📱 Office: (XXX) XXX-XXXX

📱 Office: (XXX) XXX-XXXX ext. XXXX

Note that there is an extension version and a regular version. It's quite simple really but choose the one that works best for your organization and phone structure. In the above example, you would choose one or the other. In the below example, you'd be using both the direct phone line and have an extension alternative. You might also have a third office number to include.

📱 Direct: (XXX) XXX-XXXX

📱 Office: (XXX) XXX-XXXX ext. XXXX

📱 Main: (XXX) XXX-XXXX

Its' because of this situation, where I'd shake things up a bit. For the direct phone number to your office, I'd use "Direct". For the general extension system with my extension number, I'd use "Office", and for the main organization number I'd use "Main".

The Main number is so that people can attempt to contact another person in the organization if I'm away from my desk our out of the office. I'd provide all of these numbers to show people that they can get ahold of me with many options. This is key.

Being available to your customers and co-workers is very important and cannot be stressed enough.

Mobile Phone

When it comes to adding your personal cell phone into your signature, many people shy away from it. I personally take the opposite approach and include it in every email that I send.

The reason that I include it is much like the other sections. I provide as much info as I can to ensure that the recipient of the email knows that I'm accessible to them. Regardless of whether or not I'm actually at my desk.

This helps to bring clients and customers closer to you rather than to push them away. Nevertheless, I add my cell phone number to my email signature in the same format as the other numbers.

In recent years, I've also added an icon when possible for faster identification. Long ago, I used to have separate icons for office and mobile numbers, but since I've switched to an Apple computer from PC, I found it easier to just have one icon for the phones.

📱 Mobile: (XXX) XXX-XXXX

Website

In most of the positions that I've held, I never added the website to my signature. I only started doing this for my business, because everything else was either personal or as a government employee.

In the email address section, we covered that your email address should be all lowercase, and if you need to use uppercase characters to identify specific parts of your website's Uniform Resource Locator (URL)/ website address / domain / website link, etc.

My current business is called Carbon Digital, which is a digital agency. The domain is carbondigital.us, but which is exactly how it looks in my email address. My email is jared@carbondigital.us, but that isn't how I've added it to my website line of my signature.

For reference, to go to my website you can use carbondigital.us or you can use www.carbondigital.us, and they will both go to carbondigital.us.

Notice how the actual domain isn't being highlighted by default here in the text. It works the same in our email software. So, to counteract that, I've input the www.carbondigital.us version. But I take it a step further. I use normal capitalization rules for my domain after the "www." part and before the ".us" part.

In my website line on the signature, it actually looks like this:

www.CarbonDigital.us

I do this to make it significantly easier to read for anyone attempting to read it. I already know that when they click on the link and go into the browser all of the capitalization for my domain will be removed. This just makes it easier to read within my emails.

Quote

At the start of my career, I used to find inspirational quotes and insert them here. I'd change it every couple of months. It wasn't until I started working for Honeywell that I decided to keep it simple, and just go with the Marine Corps motto of "Semper Fidelis", which means "Always Faithful".

Since that time, I've never changed it. It could be because I want other Marines out there to know that I'm a Marine as well, but at the same time, I got really tired of changing my quote. There are hundreds of thousands of quotes out there, and each one has a different meaning.

If I see a quote on someone's email signature, I'll take the time to read it and see if I like it. I actually like learning about new quotes through the normal course of life, but I'm done trying to find them and that's okay with me.

The quote section is a little piece of personalization that you can add to your email signature that doesn't tear away from the overall purpose.

Organization's Legal

There are times when your organization will mandate some legal text to be added to your email signatures. While working for the Department of Defense (DOD), I've almost always had to include the "For Official Use Only" (FOUO) statement in my emails.

The official FOUO statement is as follows:

FOR OFFICIAL USE ONLY- This transmission contains material covered by the Privacy Act of 1974 and should be viewed only by personnel having an official "need to know." If you are not the intended recipient, be aware that any disclosure, copying, distribution or use of the content of this information is prohibited. If you have received this communication in error, please notify me immediately by e-mail and delete the original message.

Depending on the size of the page, you might be able to see that there are manually added break points in the text.

It wasn't until I started building automated emails in SAS Enterprise Guide that I decided to change the way this is displayed in my signature. I used to simply add the text, and manually add the "return" to make it look like a paragraph.

When I started building automated emails, that became a pain in the butt to keep up with. I saw a co-worker's FOUO statement that had a "start" and "end" point in their email with the same text as mine and was formatted the same as my version.

I decided to take that concept, and mold it into my own. For anyone who has ever hand coded some HTML, you'll see this fairly quickly. In HTML, there is almost always a "start" and "end" piece of code. "<p>" is how you start a paragraph and "</p>" is how you end the paragraph. I decided to use this to make my own version.

THE SIGNATURE

So, I added a start and end section, and in the middle, I made the paragraph to flow on only one line. Now I'm not adding the break points manually into the text.

--------------------FOR OFFICIAL USE ONLY--------------------

This email has attached data which is subject to federal laws/regulations prohibiting unauthorized release. Such laws/regulations include, but are not limited to, the Trade Secrets Act, 18 U.S.C. 1905, a federal criminal law which can impose criminal penalties for unauthorized releases.

--------------------FOR OFFICIAL USE ONLY--------------------

This allowed me to write cleaner automated transactional emails, that took up only three lines of code, whereas my previous version took up about ten lines of code.

Since implementing this in my automated transactional emails, I've embraced this in my own email signature. I've been quite satisfied with it ever since.

When your organization mandates that you have some type of legal text in your email signature, you need to make sure that, it's not only there, but that it stands out.

At no point in time, do you want to take any blame for creating legal issues This type of format that is bold and out there will help you protect yourself.

I also make sure that the font size of the legal section is exactly the same as the rest of my email signature. You don't want to have that "small print" at the bottom of your email for several reasons, but I'll give two. These two reasons are probably the biggest to understand anyways.

The first is that the small print makes it look like you are hiding something. This is the opposite of what you want to present with your customers, so to counteract that line of thought, you make it larger and easier to read.

The second is potential legal issues. If it's hard to read in the email, someone might raise the concern that they couldn't read the legal text. While this isn't technically your problem (because they can copy/paste it into a document and make the text legible for themselves), you want to take the stance of preventative measures. Prevent the problem before it becomes a problem.

My Examples:

The following are real examples from my career. For security, I've removed some content and replaced it with an "X" in the actual signature. All of these signatures are from after my time in the Marines, but they still all show a progression through my time.

You'll notice the red phone icon. I discovered that I couldn't add an email icon in my day job, so the phone icons were removed. But you'll notice in my business email, I've included it back because I set my own rules.

Another thing that you'll notice in my email signatures is that I explicitly detail everything and try to not utilize any acronyms. This is key to making sure that everyone can completely understand who you are, and where you work.

HONEYWELL, CONTRACTOR (2012-2014)

If you have any questions or concerns, please don't hesitate to ask.

Respectfully Sent,

Mr. Ledbetter, Jared M.
Supply Technician
III MEF Support Team (Reset)
Honeywell Technology Solutions, Inc.
USMC Email: jared.m.ledbetter.ctr@XX.XX

📞 DSN: XXX-XXX-XXXX

📞 Commercial: XXX-XXX-XXXX

📞 Mobile: XXX-XXXX-XXXX

📞 Mobile from U.S.: XXX-XXX-XXXX-XXXX

🌐 www.honeywell.com

"Semper Fidelis"

FOR OFFICIAL USE ONLY- This transmission contains material covered by the Privacy Act of 1974 and should be viewed only by personnel having an official "need to know." If you are not the intended recipient, be aware that any disclosure, copying, distribution or use of the content of this information is prohibited. If you have received this communication in error, please notify me immediately by e-mail and delete the original message.

DLA EMPLOYEE-Part 1 (2015-2016)

If you have any questions or concerns, please don't hesitate to ask.

Respectfully Sent,

Mr. Ledbetter, Jared M.
General Supply Specialist
XXX Reconciliation Branch
Defense Logistics Agency, Disposition Services

📞 DSN: (XXX) XXX-XXXX

📞 Commercial: (XXX) XXX-XXXX

📞 Mobile: (XXX) XXX-XXXX

📞 Fax: (XXX) XXX-XXXX

✉ Email: jared.ledbetter@XXXX.XXXX

"Semper Fidelis"

FOR OFFICIAL USE ONLY- This transmission contains material covered by the Privacy Act of 1974 and should be viewed only by personnel having an official "need to know." If you are not the intended recipient, be aware that any disclosure, copying, distribution or use of the content of this information is prohibited. If you have received this communication in error, please notify me immediately by e-mail and delete the original message.

DLA EMPLOYEE-Part 2 (2016-2018)

If you have any questions, or concerns, please don't hesitate to ask.

Respectfully Sent,

Mr. Ledbetter, Jared
Supply Systems Analyst
XXX Analysis Team
Defense Logistics Agency, Disposition Services

✉ Email: jared.ledbetter@XXXX.XXXX

📞 DSN: (XXX) XXX-XXXX

📞 Work: (XXX) XXX-XXX

📞 Mobile: (XXX) XXX-XXX

📞 Fax: (XXX) XXX-XXX

"Semper Fidelis"

FOR OFFICIAL USE ONLY- This transmission contains material covered by the Privacy Act of 1974 and should be viewed only by personnel having an official "need to know." If you are not the intended recipient, be aware that any disclosure, copying, distribution or use of the content of this information is prohibited. If you have received this communication in error, please notify me immediately by e-mail and delete the original message.

NAVY EMPLOYEE (2018-Present)

If you have any questions, or concerns, please don't hesitate to ask.

Respectfully Sent,

Mr. Ledbetter, Jared
Supply Systems Analyst
XXX Master Data
Naval Supply Systems Command, Weapons System Support

✉ Email: jared.ledbetter@navy.mil

📞 DSN: (XXX) XXX-XXXX

📞 Work: (XXX) XXX-XXXX

📞 Mobile: (XXX) XXX-XXXX

"Semper Fidelis"

-------------------FOR OFFICIAL USE ONLY-------------------

This email has attached data which is subject to federal laws/regulations prohibiting unauthorized release. Such laws/regulations include, but are not limited to, the Trade Secrets Act, 18 U.S.C. 1905, a federal criminal law which can impose criminal penalties for unauthorized releases.

-------------------FOR OFFICIAL USE ONLY-------------------

THE SIGNATURE

CARBON DIGITAL (2017-Present)

If you have any questions or concerns, please don't hesitate to ask.

Respectfully Sent,

Mr. Ledbetter, Jared M.
Chief Executive Officer
Carbon Digital LLC

✉ Email: jared@carbondigital.us

📞 Office: (XXX) XXX-XXXX

📞 Mobile: (XXX) XXX-XXXX

🌐 www.CarbonDigital.us

"Semper Fidelis"

TEEM EMBR (2020-Present)

If you have any questions or concerns, please don't hesitate to ask.

Respectfully Sent,

Mr. Ledbetter, Jared M.
Chief Executive Officer
Teem Embr LLC

✉ Email: jared.ledbetter@teemembr.com

📞 Office: (XXX) XXX-XXXX

📞 Mobile: (XXX) XXX-XXXX

🌐 www.TeemEmbr.com

"Semper Fidelis"

CHAPTER 6

The People

Now, we'll switch gears and talk about the people being addressed in your email. There are three places to include people in the email. Those sections are the "TO", "CC", and "BCC".

The "TO" Line:

The "TO" line is who the email is being addressed to. This is NOT where you add everyone that is getting the email, just because. If you are doing that you need to stop it right now.

The most annoying thing about an email, that I've seen, is where everyone is added into the "TO" section. NO! The probability of you needing twenty people to respond or take action to one email is insanely low.

The "TO" line is specifically for those people that need to take action, review for approval, or need to respond. Everyone else needs to get moved down a line into the "CC" section.

The "CC" Line:

The term "CC" stands for "carbon copy". Anyone older than thirty, might recall that documentation used to be hand-written into forms using a pen. This ink, when writing on the form, was transferred through carbon paper onto a second or third copy. These non-original copies of the forms were called the "carbon copy".

In email terminology, the "CC" is used for informational purposes only. All of the people who aren't directly involved in the email. In the "TO" section above, it was stated that anyone who doesn't need to take action, review for approval or need to respond are moved to the "CC" line.

In a workplace setting, especially when working with other departments, you'll want to include your team lead and your supervisor. This is customary and considered to be an expectation in many cases. In reality, it's courteous to include these people from your direct chain of command.

Also, there is another piece of this that many people tend to neglect. It could be intentional, or it could be inadvertent, but either way it appears to be nefarious. The official position of government employee ethics is that you don't have to actually be doing anything wrong to get into trouble. If it looks like you are doing something wrong, then you are.

It's because of this type of mentality, that we need to ensure that all of the people mentioned in the email get "CC'd" (carbon copied) on the email. Basically, if you talk about a person, then you need to include them in the email.

Let's say that you are working for Safe Plastik, and you're the production manager in Atlanta. You've just run out of raw material. So, naturally, you'll be emailing the Transportation office and the Purchasing office to figure out when the next batch of raw material is going to show up. Without it, you're dead in the water and all production stops.

So, you'd want to email Purchasing first to make sure the product was ordered, and you would CC the Transportation office in case they already have it in transit.

You CC these people that you mention so that they can see that you are talking about them, but it goes a little deeper than that. You need to ensure that the information you are relaying is accurate at all times.

Let's say that you emailed Transportation first and asked where the shipment was, and they said they don't have any in stock or in route. You'd want to send that over to Purchasing and keep the Transportation staff in the CC block for posterity.

If that other person was the originator of this information, then they can confirm or deny what you are stating. Additionally, if they need to hop into the conversation, then they can see exactly what has been happening the whole time.

Naturally, the CC'd person probably doesn't want the fifty emails that it took to cover the information, but it would be much better to have all of the information when it's needed than to have to have track it down at the eleventh hour.

Lastly, if another person is talking about you emailing another department, and you didn't CC them on the email, then that could create problems within your department. It's likely that you weren't doing anything wrong, but the real world works of the phrase "perception is reality". By not including them in the conversation from the beginning, it gives off the perception that you'd keeping them out for a reason.

Once again, we have a preventative measure that is put in place to prevent problems before they actually become a problem.

The "BCC" Line:

The "BCC" stands for "Blind Carbon Copy". The purpose of the "BCC" line is to send an email to a person without everyone else on the email knowing about it.

For example, if you suspect something nefarious happening, and you don't want it to be known that you are reporting it to your supervisor, then you can "BCC" them. I've done this several times in the past and it always turned out badly.

Using the "BCC" is really useful. I have a buddy who uses the "BCC" to send himself a copy of every email that he sends. That way he has a running record of every email ever sent, which is highly useful when legal issues arise. The downside is that you are going to keep a copy of every email ever sent. So, it's going to take up a lot of space.

The biggest problem of the "BCC" is the one thing you can't control; the person receiving the "BCC" email. The reason that my "BCC" emails always ended up in disaster is because the person receiving the "BCC" email always decided that they wanted to join the conversation.

What do I mean by that? So, if you receive a "BCC" email, it's supposed to be "Blind", meaning that the other recipients can't see that you've received this email.

So, why on earth would you respond to that email to now show that you are here? That completely defeats the purpose of you getting the "BCC" to begin with.

Especially in situations where an investigation is going to occur, the recipient of the "BCC" needs to not respond to everyone. That is the biggest downfall in the process. It's call the "element of surprise" and you are losing it when you respond.

I've gotten to a point in my career where I'll test the waters on "BCC" recipients. Instead of using the "CC" on an email, I'll "BCC" my new supervisor to see what happens. Since I've been trying to move up the federal employee ladder really fast, I get to test this often.

I'll test it on my Team Leads, my Supervisor, and since I'm in systems analysis, the Subject Matter Experts (SMEs). So far, no one has passed the test of not responding to the "BCC" email.

That is why I've stopped using the "BCC" for most situations. If no one knows how it's supposed to work, then I'll just "CC" them instead. This is because I've dealt with too much stupid stuff to really care at this point.

Why "BCC" you if you are just going to come out of the shadows and respond? The answer is that I don't because it's a waste of time and energy. But I do give people the benefit of doubt and at least test it when a situation arises.

Multiple Actions:

There will always come a time when you need to send two emails, in response to one email, but don't want to. There is actually a solution for that. The first step is to make sure the necessary people are in the "TO" line.

When I come across this situation it always seems to be the same type of problem. I need to respond to person "A" and let them know that I'm unable to complete their request, and that it needs to go to person "B".

What I'll actually do it write the email to person "A", telling them the problem, and then I'll write the second email to person "B" in the same email. It's pretty nifty way of conserving time and space. Let me show you what I mean.

BEGIN EMAIL EXAMPLE:

Good Afternoon Mr. Jones,

Due to system limitations, I'm unable to complete your request. You will need to speak with John Smith from Accounting to process this transaction.

----- *BREAK* -----

Good Afternoon Mr. Smith,

If you would, please process the requested transaction.

END EMAIL EXAMPLE:

If you recall in the Hierarchy chapter, I mentioned in many ways that I typically utilize "Sir" and "Ma'am" quite frequently. I do this because the person that I'm responding to is the one person in the "TO" line.

In this situation above, I'm contacting two separate people. Both of them are gentlemen, and so, if I use "Sir" here it will create more chaos than is necessary. So, I will use "Mr. Jones" and "Mr. Smith" as a preventative measure so that they don't have to contact me to figure out what part of the email was intended for them.

In between those two separate emails, however, is the fun part. According to the official specification for Morse Code, ITU-R M.1677, International Morse Code, there is a code designation that is called "break". The break is used to start a new section of your message.

In movies that are set in a time when telegrams are the text messages of the time, you'll sometimes hear this being utilized as well. In these movies, you might hear the work "break" or "stop". The telegrams being sent in the United States didn't start using Morse Code, but after the communication language was built, it became the standard on this side of the pond. The Morse Code would then be transferred to paper, generally by someone using a typewriter. I've adapted this Morse Code methodology into my own multiple use emails.

You don't have to use the exact option that is displayed below, but you need to have a system in place at least. Realistically, it really doesn't matter what you use to separate the two emails, as long as you do so in a way that is clearly identifiable. My choice was 5 dashes, "BREAK" and another 5 dashes. It's short, simple and to the point.

----- BREAK -----

The dashes on each side is simply to highlight that this break in the message is there. I've been using this concept for well over a decade now, and I've never come across an issue while using it. It's become one of the most useful tools in my email tool bag.

Using this method, I'm able to clearly send out two separate emails at once, and everyone getting the email will see exactly what is being done here. Fortunately, the "Mr. Jones" in my emails recognize that they don't need to respond in most cases.

Lastly, the final piece of the multi-use email is the order of operations. The first half of the email is dedicated to respond to the person who has sent me the email to begin with. This is my response to them. During the course of that email, in the top half, I'll make sure to explain the situation but also to introduce the person in the bottom half.

Then in the bottom half, I address the new person in the conversation and task them with solving the problem for the original sender in the top half of the email.

In the example above, "Mr. Jones" would have sent me the email that requested my support. Since I was unable to support "Mr. Jones", I've addressed the issue that is preventing me from completing the task, and I've provided an alternative solution that will be handled by "Mr. Smith".

Then, after my break in the email, I've addressed "Mr. Smith", and requested that he take the specific action that I'm unable to do because I don't have the proper system roles to complete the task.

It's a really clean and simple way to "kill two birds with one stone", and the best part is that it's highly effective, and everyone can see that it works. This actually works significantly better in military based organizations, where people are familiar with official "radio talk" and Morse Code, though it's not limited to the military.

Unfortunately, I've never seen this level of communication catch on in emails. I do hope my starts to take hold one day.

CHAPTER 7

The Subject

Early on in my career, I had no idea how to effectively utilize the subject line of an email. In fact, for several months, I never even used it. All of that changed one day when I was told to not only, start using the subject line, but also to make sure that my subject line text is in "All Caps" (all letters are capitalized).

It took me several years to work out a system for using the subject line. It's rather complex at times, and I find myself second guessing myself. Even after establishing my own system. It's funny how things work out sometimes.

For my system, I've stopped using All Caps. I actually used it religiously up until about three years ago, but I've since backed off on this front. I realize that it's better for legibility to utilize camel case.

Camel case is something that I've picked up during my web development career. The purpose of camel case is explicitly to make things easier to read. The usage of it is very easy. Simply capitalize the first letter of each word. Let's look at a few examples.

All Caps:

WEATHER REPORT TODAY IS CLOUDY WITH A CHANCE OF RAIN

No Caps:

weather report today is cloudy with a chance of rain

Camel Case:

Weather Report Today Is Cloudy With A Chance Of Rain

You can easily see that the text is easier to read just by changing the methodology in how we capitalize each letter. We can actually take this a step further and add in other information or special characters. For example, let's change the camel case text to read like a publication title.

New Subject:

Weather Report Today is Cloudy with a Chance of Rain

The publisher's title gives the text more depth to the subject. This methodology can be significantly easier to read by everyone. By not capitalizing the words "is", "with", "a" and "of" we are presenting our subject in a scannable format.

The mind is a beautiful machine. Your mind can recognize the capitalized letters in this subject long before you begin to cognitively recognize what is there. When you read over this subject really quick, i.e. scanning it, your mind picks up and temporarily stores the capitalized words.

In this situation those words would be "Weather", "Report", "Today", "Cloudy", "Chance", "Rain". Even though this is not a full sentence, and even an improperly structured one at that, your mind recognizes that today's weather is cloudy with a chance of rain. All of this happens in milliseconds, long before you even recognize what is being stated in the subject.

Something as simple as creating levels for your text is highly useful. In our example above, you could even set "Today" to be all uppercase. When you do, the word "TODAY" will have the highest level and will stand out he most.

When writing an email subject, we need to understand what these options are, but also we need to utilize a combination of all text level options to create the most effective subject line. The text levels are identified below based on their hierarchy.

All Caps:

WEATHER REPORT TODAY IS CLOUDY WITH A CHANCE OF RAIN

Camel Case:

Weather Report Today Is Cloudy With A Chance Of Rain

Natural Caps:

Weather report today is cloudy with a chance of rain

No Caps:

weather report today is cloudy with a chance of rain

Now that we've covered the subject line capitalization, we can move onto the structure. For my own personal subject line system, I've broken the content down into four separate elements that are utilized when writing the subject line.

Category + Status + Reference + Date = Subject

Each of these four elements need to be in this exact order every time. Category, Status, Reference and Date. You won't have each of these elements every time you write an email. In many cases, and depending on your role in the organization, you might never get all four elements in a single subject.

Before diving into the use cases, let's cover the elements.

Category:

When it comes to the category of the email subject, I tend to utilize the "Keep It Simple Stupid" (KISS) method. Think of the category as an overall subject for the entire email. The reality is that the category is relatively subjective.

There are many different types of categories. This could range from a report or document title, or a system reference, or even a recent phone call with a client. The possibilities are endless when it comes to the category. Let's look at a few examples.

When you are sending a report, you could use the report's title. This is actually the most common usage of the category when sending a report.

When you're sending a document, you could use the document title or the purpose that the document serves. In many cases, the title of the document would coincide with the purpose of the document, which is why either should suffice.

THE SUBJECT

It really depends on how your organization is setup for these matters. In the event that the document and purpose don't have the same title, I'll tend to lean towards the document title.

Let's say you are working a system issue, and you've got to email another department for support. In these cases, I'd find a way to relay that problem in five words or less. I would also never utilize the word "glitch" when discussing system issues. There is no such thing as a system glitch. Either you have a problem, or you don't. A "glitch" would indicate improper programming on the developer's part. So, I would highlight that issue instead. If you don't know what the problem is then simply state "problem" or "issue".

In my current role, we have daily transactions that are sent manually to be processed manually. These transactions are generated by the system, and a transactional email (email sent when specific conditions are met, like a lost password email) is sent to our department. These system generated emails already have a subject, so they are routed to the proper department to work it utilizing the same subject.

When identifying departmental categories for emails, I like to think of the department tasks and workload as a pyramid. When starting a new position, I've gone as far as using Microsoft Visio to create my email hierarchy. I've also utilized Microsoft PowerPoint and Word.

Once you've established this hierarchy, follow the path all the way up to the top, then drop back down a level or two. This is generally the place you want to be for your category.

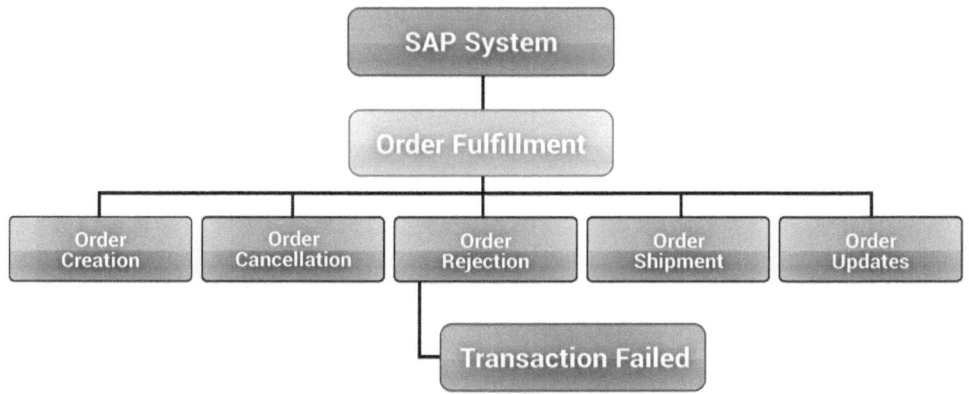

In the image above, you've got a failed transaction that you are working on. If you're unable to fix it, you'll have to send this out to another department. To find the proper subject category, look at where your problem is.

You're located under "Order Rejection", which is under "Order Fulfillment", which is under "SAP System". By moving up to the top level, you'll reach "SAP System". Naturally, in this case you will likely not want to utilize that. You'd only include this if your organization utilizes multiple pieces of software. In these cases, you could prefix the category with "SAP" to keep it simple.

Under "SAP System", you have "Order Fulfillment". I would start with this and take pieces of the remaining sub-items in the hierarchy. The subject category that I would utilize here would likely be "Order Fulfillment Rejection Failed".

This is but a simple example of how you can create your own categories to utilize in your subject line, but this part needs to be the most informative part of your subject. The more defined your category is, the clearer it will be to the reader.

Status:

The status is the next critical part of your subject line. There are hundreds of words we can utilize, but I'll name a few so that you can get the idea of what we need here.

Approved
Completed
Error
Failed
Initiated
Pending
Rejected
Requested

These are just a few of these "status" type of indicators. As stated before, there are hundreds of these. I don't utilize a status for every email. In general, I only utilize a status when discussing a system or process. During the course of regular communication with my peers, I don't have a need to utilize the status.

Since my current role is in systems analysis, I'll tend to use this more frequently than most. Nevertheless, it's important to note how these can be utilized. In the example from the category section, the category I chose to utilize was "Order Fulfillment Rejection Failed". Since "failed" was already utilized, then I've got no real need to add another status, and therefore would omit the status.

If you are working in a finance role, you're very likely to be working with financial transactions. When discussing financial transactions, you might include the status of "Paid" or "Unpaid". Even more so when you are working in Accounts Receivable or Accounts Payable. Those two "flags", if you will, are going to rule your world. To ignore them would do yourself a disservice.

Because of the "paid" and "unpaid" status, you could utilize something called an inbox rule, to highlight these emails based on a category, or even move them to a separate inbox area.

The possibilities are truly endless when you're utilizing proper email software. Most medium-sized companies and enterprises will likely be using Microsoft Outlook. Which means that this is the perfect kind of information to learn.

Reference:

The reference part of your subject can be a nice topping on the cake. We utilize the reference mostly for two reasons. The first being a quick reference to what we are talking about. The second is more for email management.

Think about this for a minute. If your role in your organization is to execute the same menial task, then all of your emails could easily look identical. This is exactly what is happening at my department for those automated system emails that I receive daily. They contain transactions, and the email subject is the same every day.

How easy would it be to get lost in these emails? It's really easy. In fact, I've got to dedicate some time to reviewing them to ensure that none were missed. I only get about a hundred of them daily, so it's not too bad. But I do need to review each one of them to ensure that none were overlooked, and this is an extremely tedious process.

Fortunately, the emails have an almost identical subject line, and they are sent from different email addresses. Because of this, I'm able to utilize inbox rules and categories to clean up the madness within my inbox.

Much of my career has been dedicated to ordering parts and equipment. Each of these orders will have an order number, and I'll use this order number in my reference part of the subject.

In my last couple of roles, I've work very intently with the "Material Master" (section in SAP that is used to manage all of the part numbers in the SAP system). Due to this role task, I'm consistently utilizing the part numbers as my reference in my email subject.

There are also times when you want to omit the reference. For example, if you've got multiple reference items, then it's pointless to add them all in the subject. In my line of work, I'm typically working with hundreds, thousands or millions of reference numbers. Because of this, there is no need to include a reference number for these situations.

The reference should only be used in those one-off situations, and not in bulk workloads. There are times when you'll need to break up your bulk workload into multiple emails, but it's really dependent on the situation.

For example, I might have one thousand part numbers on a report that need to be fixed. Each part number will have a specific program office that will need to keypunch the transactions to fix the problem at hand.

Your organization might prefer that you send one email to each of the ten program offices individually. In these situations, I'd utilize the program office as a reference point. It's because I'm going to be sending multiple emails that are identical in nature that I'll use the program office as the reference.

If at all possible, you should try to resist this type of nonsense. If there is no mandate, legal requirement or policy requirement, I'll not worry about sending those ten emails. I always try to operate off the mantra "work smarter, not harder", and I'll generally put myself in precarious situations to maintain this.

So, no, I wouldn't do this. Since we are talking about one thousand part numbers, then it would likely be in a spreadsheet. My simple solution would be to add a column in the spreadsheet and identify those program offices in the spreadsheet. Then, I'd send one mass email to everyone and be done with it. But that is me.

Nonetheless, you should always try to include a reference where possible. When you are working in bulk, you don't always need a reference, as depicted above.

Date:

The final piece of our subject line system is the date. As you may know there are plenty of way to display the date in our

THE SUBJECT

emails, documents, systems, etc. but there is only one that will consistently never fail.

In a system like SAP, you'll have dates representing August 1, 2020 to look like 08/01/2020 or even 01-AUG-2020, but neither of these will work consistently across all of your work. The format that you should be using is one that I picked up in the Corps; 20200801. This is the single best date format, and I'll show you exactly why.

Say that you have a weekly report called "Weekly Errors" and you want to use the date format of 08-01-2020. Let's look at it closely. When you have these files into a folder, here is what you'll get over time.

Weekly Errors 08-01-2018
Weekly Errors 08-01-2019
Weekly Errors 08-01-2020
Weekly Errors 08-07-2018
Weekly Errors 08-07-2019
Weekly Errors 08-07-2020
Weekly Errors 08-14-2018
Weekly Errors 08-14-2019
Weekly Errors 08-14-2020
Weekly Errors 08-21-2018
Weekly Errors 08-21-2019
Weekly Errors 08-21-2020
Weekly Errors 08-28-2018
Weekly Errors 08-28-2019
Weekly Errors 08-28-2020

You can see how this would make it complicated to find the exact report you want to locate. The month is properly filtered of course, as well as the date, but when you are locating the correct year everything is blended together. Maybe we can try the other format instead; 01-AUG-2020.

Weekly Errors 01-AUG-2020
Weekly Errors 01-JUL-2020
Weekly Errors 01-JUN-2020
Weekly Errors 01-AUG-2020
Weekly Errors 15-AUG-2020
Weekly Errors 15-JUL-2020
Weekly Errors 15-JUN-2020

Here you can see that the day of the month is the initial filter, then it's the alphabetical month. This too doesn't do well over the course of time. It's because we are using the letter abbreviation for the month. Let's look at the recommended option for both of them.

FIRST EXAMPLE:

Weekly Errors 20180801
Weekly Errors 20180807
Weekly Errors 20180814
Weekly Errors 20180821
Weekly Errors 20190801
Weekly Errors 20190807
Weekly Errors 20190814
Weekly Errors 20190821
Weekly Errors 20200801

Weekly Errors 20200807

Weekly Errors 20200814

Weekly Errors 20200821

SECOND EXAMPLE:

Weekly Errors 20200601

Weekly Errors 20200615

Weekly Errors 20200701

Weekly Errors 20200715

Weekly Errors 20200801

Weekly Errors 20200815

You can see here in both of these examples, that everything is properly sorted in chronological order every time. It's because of this that every file that is needed will be easy to fine every time. This is why I always utilize the numbered format for YYYYMMDD in all of my work. I learned this the hard way, as I'm sure many of you have experienced this.

Moving on past the elements, in the majority of my emails, I'll use the following quite frequently. There are many complex situations where I use all four, but they are rare when compared against these two. Excluding my system status emails of course.

Category + Reference + Date

Category + Date

Let's say that I have a weekly report that is run. The title of the report doesn't change, and it's utilized as the category. Yet, the data in the report changes each week, so we'll definitely want to use the date in the subject. Let's say that you are at

Safe Plastik (fake company from earlier) and the organization uses "SAP" and you are working in the Intermediate Document (IDOC) department.

An IDOC is used to transfer data between multiple systems or other modules within SAP. Each week you need to run a report to look for IDOC errors, and you've got to send that out to the team to work.

Some examples of your subject line could look like the below. If you're unfamiliar with SAP and the IDOC world, "Order Fulfillment" is generally referred to as "OF" and "Interface" is shortened down by using "INT". When you put them together in the "Reports, Interfaces, Conversions, Enhancements" (RICE) format, it ends up being OF-INT-number.

Format 1: Category
Subject: IDOC

Format 2: Category + Status
Subject: IDOC Errors

Format 3: Category + Status + Reference
Subject (long): IDOC Errors for Order Fulfillment Interface 11
Subject (short): IDOC Errors OF-INT-11

Format 4: Category + Status + Reference + Date
Subject (long): IDOC Errors for Order Fulfillment Interface 11 3-AUG-2020
Subject (short): IDOC Errors OF-INT-11 3-AUG-2020

You can see above how utilizing all four elements in your subject line can be highly effective. When I read format four from above, you can easily see how it provides exactly enough information to understand the email content without even needing to read the email.

This is your goal each time you are writing an email subject. You want to let everyone know exactly what is going on in the email without them needing to read the email body to understand what the subject of the email is.

This should sound like common sense, but I couldn't tell you how many times I've seen the email subject not being used effectively. It's one of the simplest things to do, yet many people overlook the power behind the subject line.

CHAPTER 8

The Message

The message of the email lies between the opening salutation and your email signature. This is where all the magic happens, and there is much to consider here.

The first, and most important, philosophy on the email message is to assume, or pretend, that no one knows what you are talking about. Let that sink in for a moment because it's very important. Assume that NO ONE knows what you are talking about. What purpose does that serve?

When you're in a meeting, and you are talking with someone who doesn't know what you are talking about, what do you do? Realistically, there is only one thing to do. You must educate them on the topic so that they can be part of the conversation.

The reason that this is important is quite simple. It's your job to ensure that everyone on the email fully understands what you are saying in your emails every time you send an email. When you leave questions unanswered, or people are forced to decipher your email like Egyptian hieroglyphs, you are creating more problems instead of helping to solve problems.

We don't want to create more problems. Really our intent should be to solve more problems. By ensuring that you email is explicit, you end up answering those questions before they are asked. You begin to prevent the questions from being asked because you've already answered them. Which keeps the conversation moving forward instead of having to halt the progress each time to answer questions that should've already been answered.

There is no need to begin freaking out now. I've been perfecting this for over a decade, and I still fall off the cart from time to time. This level of information being delivered is something that you'll have to strive to achieve in everything you do.

For me, this became natural early on in my career. I don't actually recall how or when I started using this concept, but it's been highly effective for me. I do recall, early in my Marine Corps career, that I would send an email with acronyms, or legacy-style coded data, and I'd consistently get questions about what those are.

Each week, I'd spend hours looking up the acronyms and coded data to answer these simple questions. The reason for this is because I took them at face value. I was told "this is the answer" and I believed them. Yet, when it came time to explain it in the email realm, that was never good enough.

THE MESSAGE

In the Marine Corps, there was always someone asking for a reference. In this environment, a reference is a publication number and a location where that information can be found. So, when I'm trying to answer the question on what that single piece of coded data is, I'd always end up having to look it up in the publications anyways and respond with the publication number and the answer's location within that publication.

Its' because of this that I actually began working out my methodology for sending emails. In the earlier versions of my system, I would get quite frustrated with other people. People who have the same job, same publications, and should use the same information have no idea what I'm talking about. This is a problem.

It got to the point where any time I'd get one of these questions, I'd stand from my desk and say "stupid" or "idiots". This became so commonplace that I needed a way to shake things up and began throwing in movie quotes to spice it up a bit. This is what paved the road for me deeply ingraining this system into my workflow.

At several times, throughout my career, I'd recommend that my co-workers and peers basically treat everyone like they are stupid. I would actually say it exactly like that "treat everyone like they're stupid". They would always squint their eyes or cock their head to the side trying to understand what I'm actually saying.

Then, I'm off the races explaining what I'm actually talking about. The concepts of being an email scientist and having the need to break all of your words down to the simplest format. Your email is the chemical compound and we are trying to find the glucose makeup for how to deliver the information in the email so that everyone can digest it on an equal playing field. The building blocks of communication if you will.

When you first start using this concept, you'll want to review your email each time you send one. Once everything is written, you need to close your eyes and take a deep breath. The purpose of this breath is to temporarily clear your mind of everything you know. When you open your eyes, you'll need to read the email as if it's the first time you've ever heard anything being discussed.

It will take time, but slowly you'll begin training your mind to see how new people will digest the information that you've written in your email. You'll begin to see whether or not you need to reword a sentence, or if you need to take out a sentence. Only with practice will you actually get to this level.

The end goal is to consistently be objective in your email communication. Being objective is when you don't include any of your feelings and opinions in your emails. The goal is to provide facts, information, questions and answers.

In many instances, I've struggled myself with remaining objective. At times, I've felt like I'm in a world full of stupid people because I can't fathom how I can be the only one to see some of the things that I've seen. It's been substantially worse when I'm in a place that has an absence of publications or a broken culture.

THE MESSAGE

I recently read *The Long Winder Trilogy* by A.G. Riddle, and now I've begun to see myself more like James Sinclair. James is the main character whose mind has surpassed everyone else around him, and because of this he is able to think outside the box, but also save the lives of his friends, family, and even humanity. It's a pretty phenomenal book, but now I'm viewing myself differently because of it. I feel I'm becoming the singularity, the anomaly that no equation can factor in. But I digress.

There are many smaller methods in our system that we can use to embrace the overall methodology in your email writing. It's not exactly the KISS method, which we'll use throughout our email writings, but it's more like the number one priority of an artificial intelligence system; like a primary directive. The rest is more of a support system to achieve said primary directive.

Let's look at some of the tools at our disposal to achieve the primary directive. We'll look at the entire list, then each one individually.

Acronyms

Dates

Letters

Numbers

References

Screenshots

KISS Method

Acronyms:

One of the most popular things in the military is the acronyms. Each agency, branch, job field, etc. has their own set of acronyms. There is most definitely a lot to take in when discussing acronyms, but the military will blow everyone else out of the water on overuse of them.

When writing publications in the military, it's a common practice to spell out the acronym first, then afterwards you can use the acronym. I've seen this being used firsthand, and I've implemented it in my own local policy and document writing for my job.

The way that you display this is simple. Let's take the KISS method. When you are using this in an email, you'll spell it out the first time, then use the acronym for the remainder of the email.

First Use: Keep It Simple Stupid (KISS)

All Subsequent Uses: KISS

When we define the acronyms that we are using, it's to ensure that there is no confusion. Like much of this book, it's a preventative measure that we use make sure that everyone is on the same page. When everyone is on the same page consistently, this will boost the level of communication and productivity throughout your emails.

Let's say that you are writing an email stating that a fellow employee needs to contact the internal CPA to review their request. If any of you have looked into finances, you'd naturally believe this to be the Certified Public Accountant (CPA). It's not hard to naturally arrive at the "accountant" form of CPA.

Yet, what you are discussing might actually have nothing to do with accounting. You could be talking about the release of images that show your manufacturing equipment. What would accounting have to do with images? The answer is more than likely "nothing". You could actually be referring to the Council of Public Affairs (CPA) in which the end result would be drastically different.

This might seem like an absurd situation, and it probably is. In my experience, I've worked for four agencies in the Department of Defense (DoD). Each of them has a different set of acronyms. There are many acronyms that are utilized in all of the different agencies, but there are also many that are new or overlap. The ones that overlap have multiple definitions for the same acronym. Which is why it's important to spell it out.

Another part of acronyms is the proper capitalization of them. For example, let's take DoD from the last paragraph. The majority of the population will use "DOD" as the acronym. While this will work, it's technically not correct. Think back to how we assign the title to books. Preposition words like "of" are not capitalized in a book title. Which is also the reason it's not capitalized in the agency name. This ultimately leads to the correct acronym of "DoD", where the letter "o" is lowercase.

Since most people (in my experience) don't really care about how things are capitalized, it's likely that no one will ever tell you this. It matters. The reason it matters is simple for me. From my perspective, if you can't get something as simple as an acronym right, then I'd be questioning your abilities. Are you really fit for that upcoming promotion if you can't use proper capitalization? Should you really be getting more customer facing duties if you can't tell the difference between an "O" and an "o"?

I know what you are thinking. This sounds like one of the stupidest things you've ever heard of, right? Wrong. In the military there is an actual phrase that encapsulates all of this into three words. For us, it's called "Attention to Detail".

The concept of Attention to Detail is simple. You actually pay attention to the details; however small they may appear. You notice it all, and you don't let anything get past you. When you get all of the little things hammered down, then you're ready for more responsibility. That next level is typically educating your subordinates on the concept of Attention to Detail. And here we have the never-ending cycle of greatness.

I personally segregate the prepositions based on usage. For example, for an actual title, I'll make sure the "o" is lowercase. For a general acronym, like COB below, I'll capitalize the "O". This is where we get to that next level of paying attention to the details, because these are general use cases, whereas a title follows the title rules.

There are several acronyms that are rather universal for me.

FYI: For Your Information

TBD: To Be Determined

COB: Close of Business

THE MESSAGE

When using FYI, it's typically for those instances when I'm just sending the email for notification or just to have. For example, if I've CC'd my Team Lead on my email, and the person who it was sent to didn't keep them on the email, I might forward the email to my Team Lead with an "FYI" notice. It's simple, and straight to the point. This also helps them manage their ever-growing inbox.

When I'm working with a process or project that doesn't have a defined timeline, but we are waiting for step "A" to be completed before we can start step "B", then I'll use the TBD in my email. That way we can all see that this needs to stay on our radar, but we don't have a defined timeline yet.

In enterprises and from software engineers, you'll hear talk of "stakeholders". The stakeholder is anyone who is directly invested in the outcome. So, a public company that you can buy stock from, those people who have purchased stock are a stakeholder. In software, however, typically the people who are affected by the changes in the software could be the stakeholders.

When you're using the TBD, you need to ensure that every stakeholder is involved so that no one is left out. Naturally, you don't have to track down everyone who bought stock, if that isn't your role. The largest use case of this is actually with software, policy and process changes.

Finally, COB is one that I picked up in the Corps. Close of Business refers to the end of the workday. If you're schedule is actually working the "9-5", then 5pm would be your COB time. The actual use of COB is relevant because each department, agency and company could be across multiple locations, multiple time zones or even countries. COB becomes a relative use. In short, as long as you finish this before you go home for the day, then you are good.

Dates:

In the subject chapter, we covered the usage of dates quite a bit. Here in the body of the email though, it doesn't matter as long as everyone can understand what the date is.

For example, if you're working with international clients, and in their country the date format used is DD/MM/YYYY, so 01/08/2020 would represent August 1, 2020, then you'll likely not want to use this date format. It would be best to use the previously recommended format of YYYYMMDD (20200801) or DD-MMM-YYYY (01-AUG-2020) instead.

It doesn't really matter what format you use here as long as everyone can understand. Because of my significant use of 20200801 format, I would likely use that date format here as well. The only time that I stray away from this is when I'm copying the 01-AUG-2020 date directly from a system and pasting it into my email.

Letters:

There will come a time when you need to highlight a single letter within the course of your email communication. It's those instances where this would apply. There are several ways to reference a specific letter, for a specific purpose, and they are all quite simple.

At one point in my career, all of our part numbers were listed in the system normally, and there was a disposal version of each part number was well. The purpose of capturing these part numbers separately was solely a financial matter. Think of a vehicle for a moment. A brand-new truck could cost you $50,000 but a used truck that was twenty years old could only be $10,000.

It's because of this that our organization decided to have a separate part number in the system for those times when a part would enter the disposal segment of the organization.

Each of these disposal part numbers were prefixed with the letter "D", which stood for disposal. In an email where you are discussing an issue with a part number, you might have to change the outcome and course correct. Sometimes this can be a simple solution, while others naturally might not be.

For example, if an employee emailed you that some of the data was wrong on a part number because of an arbitrary reason, you'd have to review the part number in question. Upon review, you discover that they are using the primary part number and not the disposal part number. You could reference this part number as such:

Please refer to the alternative disposal part number by using a prefix of "D" on the original part number.

This is simple, and straight to the point, while effectively getting the information across. That is all that we are trying to do here. Ensure that every recipient of your emails is understanding exactly what you are saying.

Say that you are referencing a publication, but you need to explicitly state which section or paragraph it's located in. Maybe it's even in a lettered appendix for the entire publication. You could easily state something like this:

Please refer to Appendix "E", paragraph 1.5, subsection (b).

This will explicitly take them to exactly where they need to be, and that is what you want. To rapid fire the information and point people in the right direction.

Numbers:

Using numbers in your email is very similar to using the letters. Using money is the simplest version of this. In the letter section above, we referenced the value of $50,000 and $10,000. Writing these values out like this is preferred because it's explicit.

Naturally there will be cases when you want to use the long version of this, but those are reserved for ballpark and general figures. For example, we sold roughly $5 billion (or $5B) worth of product this fiscal year.

Outside of using money, the remainder of use cases will revolve around inventory or a "count" of an item. There are only two real uses for using numbers in this matter. You've got the number format and the word format.

Let's say that you've got an office with ten people and two of their office chairs are broken and need to be replaced. Here are a few ways to relay this info.

Long Version: Out of the ten employees, two of them need to have their office chairs replaced.

Short Version: Out of the 10 employees, 2 of them need to have their office chairs replaced.

Based on the two above examples, I'd use a combination of both, while merging in a third method. If you've paid any attention to detail throughout this book, in many cases I'm referencing numbers in their worded format. In this context, it's a better practice to spell out the words than to shortchange myself and just use the digit format.

Yet, there are specific cases where I'll use both. Let's look at a few.

Long Version: In our department, we have two office chairs that are broken. What's the process to replace them?

Short Version: In our department, we have (2) office chairs that are broken. What's the process to replace them?

Modified Version: In our department, we have broken office chairs. See below for numbers. What's the process to replace them?

Total Chairs: 10

Good Chairs: 8

Broken Chairs: 2

Our of these three examples, I'm more prone to using the short and modified version. Most of the time, I'll use my own short version. Then when there are situations to explicitly spell out my numbers, I'll utilize the modified version.

For example, if my supervisor asked for an office chair count and note whether or not they need to be replaced. Then, of course I'll use the modified version. During the normal course of business, this would be considered overkill and not be necessary.

For the usage of a normal number, I'm placing them between parenthesis. This is done so that it's noticeable and stands out on its own. Does this mean that by not using the parenthesis, that you're doing it wrong? No, not necessarily.

Keep in mind that this entire book is completely subjective to my experiences and observations over the period of about fifteen years.

References:

Anytime that we need a reference could be a good day or a bad day depending on the actual reference itself. In the subject chapter, we discussed how a reference to an order, part number or department can provide that additional information needed to clearly determine the topic of the email just based on the subject.

Since, we've already focused on those order and part numbers, we'll move on here to focus on those times when the reference is actually a publication. Earlier, we covered how the letter can be utilized in declaration to a reference. We'll expand on that. The original version is below:

Please refer to Appendix "E", paragraph 1.5, subsection (b).

In this situation above, you could actually reference the publication number in the subject, and not have to reference it here again. Though this is possible, if you've got multiple references floating around, then it's always a best practice to include the reference number in the section declaration.

When you actually get into the habit of doing this for all of your emails, you may end up in a position where I'm currently at. Regardless of whether or not the publication was referenced in the subject, I'll always reference it again in the email body. This is a habit that I picked up throughout my career.

At one point in time, I would, almost daily, be forced into an electronic argument where I typically prevailed. These virtual wars via email consisted of policy disputes and it's because I was properly informing my peers and supervisor, that I would consistently prevail in said wars.

If you haven't learned by now, I was in the Marine Corps, and policies (including the intimate knowledge of their content) is one of the few powerful forces in nature and can make or break a mission or operation.

Using the publication numbers in your email are highly useful. Using the example before, we'll update it to include the actual reference number.

Please refer to EPUB 123.45G, Appendix "E", paragraph 1.5, subsection (b).

This level of explicit use of our organizational policy, laws or statutes, etc. can greatly influence the email recipients. By not using a reference, when you should actually include a reference, is considered neglect in my opinion.

Screenshots:

When it comes to providing a visual reference, screenshots top the cake in my opinion. I've been sending screenshots in my emails for years, but my method of sending them has changed a little over time.

Long ago, my organization didn't have the Hypertext Markup Language (HTML) version for sending emails until the past few years. It's because of this that I was only left with the plain text option. We covered this in a previous chapter, but the biggest difference is that you can have colored text, and you can include images in the body of the email.

When it comes to screenshots, I've almost always taken my screenshots and put them into a Microsoft Word document. Then I'd email that document. During the course of taking my screenshots, I'd explain what is going on, and I'd use shapes and arrows to highlight specific pieces of data to make it easier for the user to see.

In the past few years, when I've only got one screenshot to send, I've started sending that in the body of my email. That way I can scale and crop specifically what I want people to see directly in the email.

This is probably the only "shortcut" I've taken on screenshots. Which includes by extension how I actually take the screenshot. I know many people who use a tool like SnagIt, or the Snipping Tool, etc. and it's almost always a bad idea. I personally utilize the default system screenshot or "print screen" option that is available.

Many people don't understand how to scale an image, up or down, and maintain the proportions. What am I talking about here? When you are in Microsoft Word, and you've just pasted in your screenshot, you will hover your mouse over a corner and change the size.

When you change the size, if the side and top of the image don't move at exactly the same speed, then you are distorting the image. When I scale and crop screenshots, I make sure that I'm consistently scaling the image while retaining those proportions. Otherwise, it's pointless to even take a screenshot to begin with.

KISS Method:

The Keep It Simple Stupid (KISS) method is something we tell ourselves in order to remember to keep the information simple. In the Marine Corps, we called the act of using the KISS method "breaking it down Barney style". For those of you who don't remember, Barney was a purple dinosaur on a kid's television show.

Therefore, "breaking it down Barney style" meant that you would break down the complexities of the content so that a five-year old could understand what you were talking about. Of course, when you are talking about complex weapons systems that is next to impossible, but you want to at least try to keep things simple as much as possible. That's where this "Barney style" comes into play.

Using my primary directive above, the KISS method is a natural complimentary component. When you believe that everyone has no idea what you're talking about, you will naturally be forced to break down the content into sizeable chunks. Thus, you are effectively breaking it down Barney style. Which is the overall goal for the delivery of your message.

When we combine all of these elements with the primary directive, we will then be consistently delivering information at one of the highest levels possible. Focusing solely on the task at hand and achieving greatness within the click of a button (send button).

CHAPTER 9

The Tone

When you are writing your emails, there is one piece that is more important than all the rest; the tone. You could screw up everything else prior to this, but as long as you are getting the tone right, I'd call that a win. It's still not up to par for my standards (as they are extremely high), but it would be a solid step in the right direction.

In today's digital world, one of the hardest things to decipher from written text is the tone. You ever get on social media and see that one person writing in All Caps. Then someone will respond to the effect of "why are you yelling at me?" Yes, typing with your Caps Lock button on is something that will infuriate many.

It's because of that simple fact that deciphering text has multi-tiered complexities, that we need to take extra precautions to ensure that everyone reading our emails can consistently get the same message. Once again, we are off to the races with another preventative measure.

The negative tone is driven solely by our emotions. If we fail to keep our emotions in check while we are writing our emails, then what's the point of writing them to begin with. Let me elaborate.

Let's say that you have one guy in your office who asks the same questions almost daily and seems to always need help with his work. Over the course of time, there can only be one outcome to this if he never improves; you're going to snap. It's not a question of if, but a question of when.

Right now, it's August 2020, at the "rebirth" of the coronavirus pandemic. Naturally, out of everyone who still has a job, we are mostly working from home. Instead of getting those questions face-to-face, and you having to control your facial expressions, you're now more likely to get an email with these questions.

Being able to control your emotions in this situation is more important than ever. With a world set on optics, you need to be on your toes "24/7". It doesn't matter how many times this guy asks you the same question repeatedly. When you release your fury on him, you will always be at fault. Regardless of whether or not it's justified.

You have to control your emotions at all times. There have only been a handful of times that I recall letting my emotions get the best of me. They were all justified, of course, but it didn't matter because I'm an adult and I should act like one regardless of how everyone else acts.

It's my responsibility to maintain a high standard of professionalism because I'm the face of my department, and my organization, whether I want to be or not. That's where the phrase "Perception is Reality" comes back to haunt us.

Over the course of my career, there are easily hundreds of emails that I've started and never sent. That or they were modified before they were actually sent.

Anytime you begin writing, whether it's an email or even this book you're reading now, the first draft always comes from the heart and filled with emotion. That's how we are wired, and that's how the words flow out of us more fluidly.

The difference between the majority of the rest of the world and me, is that I actually revise my email as many times as it takes to get the tone and content right. I've spent ten minutes writing up a passionate email, only to spend an hour critiquing it, and perfecting it to the point where none of my emotion is present anymore.

I don't care who you are. This is something that we all need to do, if we aren't already doing it. I couldn't begin to tell you how many times I've received an email that was written in pure emotion. In my younger days, I was bold enough to respond with my own emotions.

Throughout time, I've learned that I don't have to actually respond to those emails. For the past several years, I've not responded to these emails. Even more so when I've got a supervisor who is supportive of me. When you have a boss that really cares, and has your back, it's a world of difference.

I've got no problem forwarding those emotional emails to my boss (and possibly the equal opportunity office), the sender's boss, and let him or her know that I'm not dealing with this until they calm themselves down, act like and adult, and show some professionalism.

It's not unrealistic to expect a person to show common courtesy and a bare minimum level of respect in the workplace. I don't care who you are, because I'll tell you exactly how it is, and you won't like it.

If you are the sender in this situation, it really will take some time for you to recognize your faults. There is no need to beat yourself up if you are "that guy" kind of emailer. (That guy is a reference to the military guy who gets drunk and does stupid stuff).

By no means am I claiming that I'm perfect in all that I do, but I do recognize my limits and note where I need improvement for myself. That's all that I'm proposing to each of you reading this now. There is a saying that goes something like "in order to solve any problem, you must first recognize that there is one".

I'm asking you to look and see if you've got a problem, and regardless of where you are at, to find a way to make yourself better. Once you overcome the hurdle of emotional recognition in your emails it's easier to move onto other areas.

I've been known to revise my emails several times before getting them right. I've even asked co-workers, Team Leads, and at times my supervisor to ensure that my email message is the best possible version that it can be.

THE TONE

In fact, when you are first beginning to apply these principles in your own email writings, it's best to "bring a friend". Naturally, you won't have the luxury of asking your Team Lead, or your supervisor to review every email that you send. But if you've got a friend who sits next to you, having them glance over your emails to make sure that you aren't about to drop a "nuclear bomb" via email is a good practice.

When I first started censoring my emails, or even attempting to make them better in general, I would always ask two people to review my emails and verbally "sign off" on them. I'd ask a peer to review my email, then I'd ask someone the next level up (which was typically someone with a higher rank than me in the Marine Corps).

I would do this quite frequently when I first started getting caught up in having somewhat disrespectful email communication with someone significantly higher up the totem pole than me. So, all of that drastically changed and I've since charted my own path to eventually writing this book even.

You may be wondering if there is something, we can use to keep us on track when writing out our emails. The answer is yes. I use the DIRE method.

The Direct, Inform, Refer and Execute (DIRE) method is a form of communication that will help to keep your emotions out of the equation. I already understand that many people won't be able to keep up with this type of communication, but it's definitely worth noting.

Direct:

The Direct portion refers to how you should communicate with people. You should communicate in a direct manner. Being direct doesn't mean that you have to be insensitive, but you'll definitely come across people who are overly sensitive, and they will either fear you, or they will challenge you in ways that you can't imagine.

My direct nature has gotten me into trouble on many occasions, and not for the reasons you may think. Being direct doesn't give you a hall pass to be an asshole to everyone. It doesn't. It merely refers to the fact that you are getting straight into the facts without any of the fluff.

There isn't any emotion in the fact that if you are speeding on the highway. You are significantly more likely to get a ticket and that is solely because you chose to not follow the law. Does that make it the police officer's fault that you were being stupid? No.

Facts, data, policy and system requirements, etc. aren't subjective. They are objective and care nothing about your emotion. By focusing solely on these facts, you are more likely to have a better conversation and ultimately get more work done amongst your peers and co-workers.

The challenge comes when your organization doesn't have the policies to support your workload. In these rare cases, there are only two options. More than not, a combination of both of these would be the best approach.

Option 1: Write an internal policy supporting your workload, claims, position, etc. As long as the content of the policy, and the policy itself can be perceived as objective, then this will hold for a time. It's when you cross that emotional barrier that these internal (or local) policies fall to pieces fairly easily. I've broken a few of them myself, so I'm aware of how that can go sideways for you fairly easily.

Option 2: You have to take a hard stance on where you are. If your convictions are so strong, and there is no policy supporting something that is the right thing to do, then taking a stance is one of the few options left on the table for you.

Let me explain what I'm talking about here so that there is no confusion. I don't care what your political beliefs are, your world view, or any other justification you can think of to incite problems on a political nature. I'm merely talking about process or procedure.

In 2011, I told a grown woman (an elder to me) that I would punch her in the face if she didn't stop what she was doing. This was simply because my convictions about the issue were so strong, I felt I had to take a stand. Let's go through the back story so you have some context.

In 2010, I received my Honorable discharge from the Marine Corps. During that time, I'd been in charge of multi-million-dollar accounts (we're talking $70 million or more), managing their inventory, ordering equipment and parts, and never losing track of any equipment. Ever.

In late 2010, just two months after separating from the Marine Corps, I was dropped off at the homeless shelter. There is quite a story behind my buildup, but I'll skip to the part that matters in this story.

Around August 1st in 2011, I was offered a permanent position as a receiving warehouseman in a helicopter manufacturing facility. My role was simple. Bring all the parts into my area, inventory them, process the receipt transaction, put the parts on the shelf, and when necessary issue those parts out to the production like to be manufactured.

I've had plenty of experience with all of this, but I was unfamiliar with SAP during these days. My supervisor had showed me how to receipt for parts and put them on the self in the system. So, that is exactly what I did. I wasn't but a few days into my new permanent job, when I encountered a problem.

My "warehouse" was a square that was taped to the floor, and a ten-foot caged fence. You could easily climb over it if you wanted, but when I got there, you'd have to get past me first. Before my arrival, it was a common practice for the demand planners to issue the parts to the production line once they were received in the system.

Three days into my tenure, a lady in her mid-forties walked around the corner into my area with a key in her hand. She made a beeline for my warehousing cage, and nonchalantly told me she was grabbing some parts. I was on my feet and headed to intercept when I saw where she was headed.

When she was less than a foot from the locked gate, I put myself between her and the gate to my warehouse. Again, she iterated that she was here to pick up some parts. To which my reply was something to the effect of "I've not heard anything about it". I told her once again that she wasn't getting into my warehouse.

Naturally, since I'm the new guy, she is thinking that I don't know how things work here. She proceeded to reach the key under my arm open the door that way, to which I had a simple response. "If you open that door, I will punch you in the face." Taking a step back, she scoffed at me. "You would…you would punch me in the face over this?" My single word reply said it all. "Yes".

She stormed off yelling at herself and saying she was going to tell my boss and all of those good comments you could think of during a time like that. So, I went back to work. It wasn't about ten minutes when my boss came strolling by and asked me about it.

I told him straight up, "Yes, I said that to her." To which, he was actually impressed that I wasn't a week on the job, and I cared enough about my area that I would take that strong of a stance. Then he showed me how to issue the parts to the production line and all was well. And no one ever tried to enter my warehouse cage again without my prior approval.

Now, I can see the wheels turning as you read this. They are turning in my head as I write this, and I'm wondering how many of you think I'm crazy right now. The reality is that I'm not crazy. I'm insanely dedicated to the success of the mission.

That's the difference between a work-related stance and some political crap you may choose to bring into the office. As crazy as my stand as the "gates of receiving" may seem to people, it actually goes to prove that there is a place for you to take a stance.

You see, no one told me that all of the demand planners have a key to my warehouse and were authorized to go into my warehouse cage to look for physical parts, for the purpose of creating an "order" for me to issue parts to the production line.

Also, because the company had a long stint without a warehouseman before my arrival, these demand planners had verbal approval to issue the parts themselves. And none of this was relayed to me.

Since I'm fully unaware of all of this, I was merely restoring order. And that's exactly how it was perceived by my supervisor. One that worked in my position in France for years, before getting promoted to the level where he was at. So, I'm almost positive that he'd seen this before. And he supported my decision.

When you take a stance on something like this (non-political), and you are in the right, you will almost always be justified. In my situation, I was simply told that it might not be a good idea to hit people, but that protecting my warehouse cage was justified.

The fun part in all of that is relaying that information into your emails. In these situations, I will apply the KISS method as hard as possible. Here is an example or two:

Example 1: (I've definitely got the ability to do this in the system, but my role is to maintain information. Not create information)

I apologize for the inconvenience, but you'll have to talk to the program office and see what the process is to get this part number added to the system.

Example 2: (I've definitely got the ability to do this in the system, and there are no policies preventing me from creating the order)

I apologize for the inconvenience, but you'll have to talk with purchasing to get that order created. I don't have the authorization to create an order for any reason.

In these two examples above, I know for a fact that I've got the system roles that will allow me to execute these two transactions. I also know deep down that my job is to make sure the data is correct, but I've got nothing to do with creating a part number or an order. There are other offices in my organization whose sole purpose in life is to execute those functions.

By directing the customer to the proper people, I'm also forcing those departments to do their jobs. Which, if a culture is broken, this could easily be overlooked when there are organizational problems.

Inform:

One of the elements of being direct is to present the facts. The Inform segment is no different. In fact, the "direct" and "inform" are so connected that they typically go together. When you inform people, and you are direct, you are achieving both of these at the same time with a single set of information.

The purpose of informing your email recipients is part of an effort to educate them on the topic or situation at hand. This, once again, ties back to those preventative measures that we take to prevent problems before they arise.

If you've ever taken a speech class in college, you'll know there are informative and persuasive speeches. The informative speech is solely to deliver the information, and in many cases, while creating a call to action based on that information.

When you deliver these speeches, just as you do in your email communication, you want to ensure that you leave no questions unanswered. This is something that will take years to perfect, so don't worry if you can't get this worked out on the first day.

Being able to understand the recipient of your email (anyone from co-workers, customers, clients, business partners, etc.) is nothing more than observation in the workplace. You will have to pay attention to how people receive your message. See how they ask questions based on your writing, how they respond, and ultimately, their reaction. It takes time to observe how people react to your email long before you understand how to answer their questions before they are asked.

If you can't get this right on day one, don't sweat it. This took me years to perfect myself. Only time and experience can help you out on this one, if you are willing to put in the time to make it happen.

Of course, there are things that you can do to ensure that you are on the right vector. Before sending your email, simply ask yourself, "is this fact or opinion"?

Refer:

In everyone's career, you'll definitively come across a time when you have to forward the email to another person to be worked. Whether it's a system issue, wrong department, or even outside the scope of your billet, there will come a day when you'll have to refer someone to another person, department or agency.

When you have to refer a person outside of you (your billet, office, department, agency, etc.), you'll always apologize that you can't help them, then give then the direct information that is needed to move forward.

In two examples from the "direct" section, you'll notice that I've done just this. I apologized for the inconvenience, then directed them to where they need to go, and what they need to do. It's really that simple.

Fact – I'm sorry, I can't help you.
Fact – This is the reason why I can't help you.
Fact – This is what you need to do to fix the problem.

In situations like these, you need to become the family doctor who just found out their patient has cancer. You can be sympathetic to their situation, but you need to also remember that you are just a family physician (regular medical doctor), and not the oncologist (doctor that specializes in cancer).

When you do discover that your patient has a condition outside of your ability to help them fix, you are only left with one option; a referral. It's because of this that you need to remain calm when you deliver the news. Yes, it's your job to still deliver the news even though you are unable to help them.

"I'm sorry, but we found a tumor. It looks like we caught it early, but I must refer you to an oncologist for proper diagnosis and follow on care".

Now, I'm probably legally obligated to state that I'm not a doctor, or something of that nature. But that doesn't change the fact that this is how a doctor will attempt to communicate the message. Straight and to the point. Stick to the facts of the case.

When we refer someone outside of us, this is equally important to do. We must stick to the facts of the situation, and make sure we direct them to the right people that can help them the most.

Execute:

I've always thought of the "Execute" section as being the simplest of all the DIRE elements. The Execute element is always referencing work that has been done, or needs to be done, or a combination of both.

I'm currently in a position where I have to work tickets for other customers. Fortunately, I don't have to monitor these tickets within our ticketing system, but when I need to be involved, I'm notified via email. When I work these tickets, it's always based on one of two factors. Either I need to research a problem, or I need to fix a problem.

Fixing the problems for these customers is sometimes complex, but that doesn't have to complicate my email response. I couldn't begin to describe how many times I've seen co-workers or other departments overcomplicate things.

You'll get too much info, or they are off in left field talking about something that has absolutely nothing to do with the ticket that was submitted. At times, I even wonder how some people get their jobs. Yes, it does get that bad sometimes.

When you need to respond to the ticket, and let the customer know that the work has been completed, it's the easiest email that you'll write all day. Let's say that I received a ticket were the conversion rate for a part number needs to be updated.

We all know that 1 Foot (FT) is equal to 12 Inches (IN); 1 FT = 12 IN. In our ticket, someone has fat fingered a transaction. Fat fingering means that someone has entered an erroneous number for the "IN" section. In our example the conversion currently says "1 FT = 21 IN". That is obviously wrong and needs to be corrected.

Naturally, I'd have to change that from "1 FT = 21 IN" to show a correct conversion rate of "1 FT = 12 IN", and then notify the customer that the change has taken effect. Notifying them is the easiest part.

Email Example:

As requested, part number [insert number here] has been updated to reflect 1 FT = 12 IN.

That's it! You don't have to get fancy with this and start writing a novel to them to explain how the sun rises in the east and sets in the west. You just deliver the facts in a plain and simple way. Every bit of this embraces the KISS method.

Fact – You requested this change.

Fact – The change is done.

The "As requested" is something I use almost every day. Another highly useful shortcut bit of text is "Per our conversation". Just like "As requested", I'll start the email like this and make sure that everyone knows that we have spoken on the phone or via chatting tools.

This is insanely useful, especially for follow ups. If I've reached out to you via phone or chat and we spoke briefly, this is a quick down and dirty way to get the reminder out there. When the whole premise is that I'm still waiting on you to provide or do something, this is too simple.

Example:

Per our conversation, I'm just following up for a status on "X".

I couldn't tell you how many times I've used "As requested" and "Per our conversation". It's in the hundreds of thousands. This is what you would call my bread and butter. I've used this so much that it's natural for me to use this. I've even caught myself trying to say more, and I'll start over and keep it short and sweet.

Alongside the DIRE method, you're going to need to pay attention to what you are writing and what emotions are present in the email you write. The hardest thing you'll learn in this book is the fact that you need to control your emotions.

If Microsoft Outlook had version control (storing of each version) for emails, you'd be baffled by how many versions of each email I actually have. For me, it's about writing the perfect email each time you place your hands on the home row keys.

Writing the perfect email doesn't have to take months to craft. You can do it in under fifteen minutes each time. That's not me saying that each email you write will take fifteen minutes. No. There are many emails that you will write, that simply fall into the DIRE method (especially the ticket example from the Execution element) and are easy to accomplish.

It's also important to note that there will come a time when you are challenged emotionally via email. It's not a matter of "if" it's going to happen, but a matter of "when" and "how many times" it will happen.

When this happens, there is only one way to properly get rid of those emotions so that you can write a proper email. You have to write the email emotionally. Note that I didn't say "send", only "write".

I created a bad habit of using the "CTRL + Enter" buttons on my keyboard to execute the sending of the emails that I write.

While this is a great shortcut to learn (for Microsoft Outlook), it also became my demise on several fateful days.

There have been times where I've written the entire email emotionally, and it typically looks like I've written a novel. Times that I've been on such a roll with my typing flow that as soon as I've finished writing the email, my fingers slip down to the CTRL and Enter buttons before I've realized what has happened. Let's just sum that up to "I haven't been fired, yet" from sending out an email like this, but I've definitely been in hot water.

While I still use "CTRL + Enter" to actually send my emails, I have learned to stop myself so that I can review the email before sending it. The best defense against this has been to write my email separately. Depending on the situation, I'll write in a new email or a Microsoft Word document.

Early on, when trying to fix my emotional issues in email writing, I'd open up a new email and not add any people to it. That way if I tried to send the email when I was done writing, I'd get a notification that this email isn't addressed to anyone yet.

This was huge for me because it afforded me the ability to revise my email where need be. Which prevented me from releasing my rage and fueling the fire of hatred. While not everyone out there may have the same level of anger issues as me, you're still prone to writing an emotionally charged email. Which is the opposite of what you need no matter how you want to look at it.

Whenever I write an email, I will always write it in the most natural form. Just like writing a book or a college essay. The first draft is always your natural self. Then you'll go back afterwards and proofread your work.

It's no different with emails. The only difference is that there has never been a standard on how you should write an email. There has never been a college course on writing an email. There are plenty on creative, technical and business-related writings, but nothing regarding how you should actually write up the email.

That is exactly how this book came to pass, by filling the void.

When you proofread your email prior to sending it, there are several things that you want to look for so that you can perfect the email's tone; emotion, grammar, simplicity and the DIRE method. Naturally, following the DIRE method from the beginning is going to be beneficial to your writings.

When it comes to grammar, you just want to utilize your language's proper grammar rules. I don't pretend to be a Subject Matter Expert (SME) in the English language, nor do I have a degree in English or anything close. I just observe and pay attention.

If you've got a problem with grammar, you can write your emails in Microsoft Word and the software has a "spell check" feature, but it will also show you (while you are writing) where your spelling and grammar errors are at. Alternatively, if you're looking for something a little more high-speed and modern, you can look into a tool like Grammarly. I've used Grammarly before and it's a simple tool with lots of grammar-related benefits.

Outside of those generic transactional emails (see DIRE method, execute element), I'm most likely writing multiple versions of my email. The first draft is always something that just flows out of me. And I let it flow naturally. The purpose of this is to get those juices flowing, but also if I'm emotionally charged, it's to get all of that initial emotional response out of my system.

Too many times in the world, people will respond with their first thought. You can easily see this on social media, when people comment with some of the vilest and emotionally charged content you'll ever consume on the internet.

We have to retrain ourselves. The purpose of this "reeducation" is to give us that brief moment of clarity just before hitting that send button. If you could've had two seconds of thought prior to sending that "one" email, how better off would you be right now?

It's happened to us all. We've all sent at least one email, that we knew instantly as soon as it was out, that we just made a mistake. So, we search out inbox looking for that email only to seek out a way to retract the email before the reader sees it. You haven't been the first to make this mistake, and you won't be the last. But you can learn from it.

Anytime you've got to send an email, you should always take a quick glance just before actually sending the email. It could save your job, your livelihood and even your career.

At times, I've been so blinded by my emotions, that every time that I've revised an email it never seemed to be good enough. What do you do in those situations? You phone a friend.

I couldn't even begin to quantify how many times I've asked a co-worker, friend or leader to review my email for the purpose of making sure it was the best version it could be. It's definitely pushing one thousand. This is more complex in this remote (coronavirus) world, but it's still doable.

Even since starting to write this book, I've asked for help reviewing an email. It's not that hard to ask for help and asking for help will keep you humble. So, it's what we could call a "win win".

Naturally, I'd prefer to be in my office cubicle and ask a neighbor for help reviewing my email, but in today's remote world that likely isn't an option for most of us right now. You can simply send them an email with the content of the email and ask them if it looks and sounds good. This is even easier when you are already writing the email in Microsoft Word. That's because there is a simple way to share the Word document in an email as an attachment. File > Share > Email > Attachment. Done.

You could even use your organization's internal chat software and send the email content there. I've used this exact method many times in software like Skype. It's too easy to get their attention. "Hey, do you have a second to review my email? I want to make sure it is worded correctly." Then you can copy and paste the email, or even upload the Word document.

It's too simple of a process for you to "phone a friend" and ask for their help. I would even go as far to say that if you neglect to do this, and your email comes off as unprofessional or emotionally charged, then you don't really care about your job, your supervisor, the image that you present as an employee of the organization, or being a professional.

That's exactly right. You don't care. And if you don't care, then I (as your supervisor) wouldn't care if you retained employment or not. Of course, that isn't the first thought from you sending one bad email. It's never been a question of if you will make mistakes. You will definitely make mistakes. It's always a matter of how you will handle them, and how you will learn from them and improve yourself as a result of your mistake. I'll never fault anyone for making a mistake. If you fail to learn and grow from it, that will always be your fault.

What I'm saying here isn't that you're definitely going to get fired from one unprofessional email. Well, actually it's possible. I'll put it like that.

There will always be an organizational culture where you can get fired if you make a big enough mistake. These business owners who are driven by the next series of profit margins and focus on their own achievements instead of the team's achievements will likely be the ones that fall into this category. Another tell-tell sign is when these leaders take credit for the team's work.

THE TONE

In many cases, these types of leaders will always blame you for your mistake, and they will never take ownership of it. Most of the time, they also won't try to fix the problem. Even though making mistakes is the greatest teacher you could ever have.

The reason that this is important to note is because you may be working for an organization or leader who thinks and operates exactly like this. You might be working in a culture that is toxic to the employee base. In your single moment of emotionally charged weakness, you could send the wrong email to the wrong person and have it all blow up in your face.

You could've sent that email to a client who is responsible for twenty-five percent of the organization's annual revenue, and because of your unprofessional email, the client has decided to take their business. Effectively crippling the entire organization because the business owner just happened to take more withdrawals than making investments.

So now, not only you job will be on the line, but half of the company will be on the fence as well. In that perfect storm type of combination, your email could be the catalyst that is responsible for the collapse of an entire organization. Since the organization you work for already has a bad culture, you'll most definitely get the blame. Regardless of those other (more significant) factors that led to their demise. Good luck finding your next job, because that "referral" from your last boss will be interesting to say the least.

You're probably thinking that I'm crazy because this could never happen. It actually could happen. This example is really over the top, and the probability of it actually happening like this is relatively low, but anything could happen in our world.

For a little over two and a half years, I was a government contractor employee. My role within "Supply" was to order all of the parts needed, process the receipt transactions in the system, and track every penny in our $1.6 billion budget.

Each month, I would get an email from the Financial Data Manager (FDM), and she would ask me for the documentation showing that we've physically received and receipted for parts. Should would actually never look at what I've done in the system and would simply export the report on her financial side and send it to me blindly.

I would have to respond to this email each month and provide the documentation showing that we've received and receipted for the orders in question. It wouldn't be for all orders, as we always had open orders, but our order volume was really high. This left me with finding all the paperwork for all of our closed orders because they wouldn't accept the spreadsheet that I used to track every penny.

Each time, I would have to send these PDF files to this finance lady with all of our documentation. Well, eventually I got to a point where I've decided to be proactive. So, each week I started emailing her the documentation with my tracker spreadsheet. The purpose of it was to send her about twenty or more files each week, instead of having to track down hundreds at a time.

Several months go by, and I'm still getting these same emails from her because she hasn't taken any of the paperwork that I've sent her and updated her side. From the start of my career up until this point, this had been one of the worst moments I'd ever had.

That was the day that I snapped.

I proceeded to formulate my response. I added the last several weeks of emails that I'd sent her. I was fueled by nothing more than pure hatred for this woman and her inability to do her job properly. I mean, I'd provided her each week with exactly the proper documentation that she needed because I used to have to do this when I was in the Marine Corps.

I wrote my mini novel in email form, and I was effectively sealing my fate for the future on this one. Destined to be that one prisoner who spends their entire prison sentence in solitary confinement. I had condemned her for being incompetent in her work because I had received read receipts (proof that she had received and read my emails) and provided them in the email response as well.

I also made sure to CC (copy) her supervisor on the email. It was important for him to know that this employee is doing nothing for a whole month and expecting me to fill in the gaps of her work. Needless to say, I was fueled by a lot more than hatred at this point. Yet, the result was not as I'd expected it to be.

The only expectation that I had was that this supervisor would investigate the problem and address it with her. Little did I know that he would never "hear" me because I'm nothing more than a measly contractor. I'd expected to get into trouble, but I also expected my problems to go away.

They didn't. In fact, they worsened.

It was at that point where I began to realize how the world works. You see, that financial lady responded to me, basically saying "I'm a federal employee, and you don't talk to me like that." To which my reply was simply, "I'll say what I want, especially if you aren't doing your job."

Again, I must reiterate that I had reached my breaking point with this person over the course of several months, including my proactive work to prevent these emails from even coming in. Those emails never stopped.

After her supervisor sided with his employee, naturally, I was immediately accosted for sending such a brash and disrespectful email to her. Twice.

Unfortunately, and probably for the better, I wasn't fired. In fact, my supervisor at the time became the new middleman between her and I. Since I'd copied him on every one of those emails, over the course of several months, he knew exactly what kind of effort I'd put into keeping the financial team ay bay.

He wasn't as upset as I expected him to be. He knew and told me that my intent was spot on, but he also knew and mentioned that I shouldn't have worded my email the way that I did. This was my learning experience that could have ended severely badly. Being a government contractor, that federal employee supervisor could've easily demanded my job. And he would've likely gotten it.

When you let your emotions drive your typing, everything can go sideways really, really quickly. It's important for each of use to be vigilant in recognizing when we need to reword our email. In many cases, those emails that are emotional are simply for us to feel better about the situation.

We don't need to tell the other person how we feel. In fact, it's best that we don't, because the level of professionalism that is needed constantly can be achieved. You just have to simply seek to attain it. One day at a time. One email at a time. You can achieve near perfection, but you'll have to keep track of it.

We are all flawed as humans. I'm quick to tell the world how I've made mistakes because I want other people to learn from them. And yet, no one seems to be paying attention.

I truly hope everyone reading this will see the message that I'm putting on display here. We can all do better, and we should all strive to be better.

Better people.

Better writers.

Better professionals.

CHAPTER 10

The Reply

The original design for this book included a significant part of the technology side of email management. Much of that was taken out and condensed into only the necessary parts. One of those parts is the "Reply" button.

If you've utilized an email address for any length of time, you'll notice that there are two types of replies that you can do. This is mentioned because I've seen too many people do this wrong. And yet this is really, really simple.

The standard reply should be "Reply to All". I actually use this so much that I'll catch myself trying to use it when I'm writing an email with one person. This is the most important header button you'll ever use. This is the "standard reply" that you should be using for almost EVERY situation.

If you are about to reply to an email with several people on the distribution list ("TO" and "CC"), then there can be only two reasons why you would deviate off of the standard reply.

The first reason is that you want to send the email to one person. In which case, you could also use the "Forward" button. The second reason is that you are trying to hide something. Unfortunately, there is a third reason. In reality, many people appear to "forget" that the Reply to All button even exists.

There have been instances where I have taken an email with ten people on it and send an "offline" email (so it's not in front of the masses) and used the single "Reply" or "Forward" button. This is a tactical move to pull out of your toolbox when needed. The purpose is typically to get some insight on a subject before responding to the entire group. I even applaud this tactic when used properly.

I couldn't begin to quantify how many times I've received an email on the second reason. When working with a co-worker that I was training, he would consistently never use the Reply to All button. Never. I would always have to add the other team members on the email traffic, and this becomes really annoying when you are doing this daily. I've even picked up the phone, or walked to his desk, and told him straight out that he needs to use the Reply to All button.

Another important piece of the reply is restructuring the distribution of recipients. Over the years, and in my current role, I will see everyone added into the "TO" line. The reality of the situation is that not everyone needs to interact on the email, and some people are getting the email for informational purposes only.

I will actually take the time to restructure how the recipients are listed. Almost all of the people will get moved to the "CC" line, and only the people that I'm addressing in the email will remain in the "TO" line.

It's sad to say that this is necessary, but it really is for continuity of information. When you look back on these emails six months from now, you will need to verify that person "A" received it. This will make it easier to identify them quicker, especially if they should have been in the "TO" line.

The last replay factor that I'll leave you with is removing or adding people within the distribution. When replying an email, there are many instances where you'll want to include your Team Lead or Supervisor. They may not need to be involved, but you want them to know what is going on.

This is especially useful when working with other departments. You can show your leaders that you are working cordially with other departments and making good things happen for both departments. Many leaders want to know that you can work with other areas of the organization. In most places there is a "communication" level requirement in the job description.

At times, you'll even have to remove people who are irrelevant to the conversation. When removing people, you want to ensure that you aren't taking someone off that should remain. This is even more critical when working with other departments.

When you remove people, you need to remember that you aren't the only two people on the email (you and the other main person). This other main character in the email may add their co-workers or leaders on the email too. You will most likely want to keep these other related personnel on the email.

The biggest thing to remember is that only relevant personnel should be on the email to begin with. A couple of weeks ago, I received an email with a few people on it. I was asked to execute some work that was outside my lane. The email came to me because my Team Lead told them to contact me.

It turned out that one of my co-workers was on leave (vacation time), and it was routed to me to backfill that workload. The problem was multifaceted though. I was not able to fix the problem for them because I didn't have the knowledge of that role, but I also didn't have the system roles to execute that functionality. Which was a problem for them.

Additionally, the main problem was that the data between this system and another didn't match. My department's role is that of a data synchronization function, and not the data integrity function. Meaning that we work the system areas that send data back and forth between these two systems, but we have no idea on how to verify if the data is accurate.

I called the customer to get some feedback and make sure I understood what he was asking. The customer was asking for me to verify that the data was correct and asked that I fix it for him. Since this is outside my knowledge and capabilities, I recommended him to another department who focuses on that data verification part. He completely understood that I wouldn't

THE REPLY

be able to help him today, and also agreed that this work should be sent out to another department.

When the email came back to me the next day, it was full of surprises. Not only did the customer not fully understand what my response was, he was trying to push it back on me as to say that I never helped him out on the first email. To make matters worse, he copied two supervisors from different divisions that were three levels up from where I was at.

Effectively, this guy put me on the spot, and by the way his email was worded it's clear that this was his intention. He was trying to get me to do the work instead of having the right people do it. That actually happens a lot in my organization, so it wasn't a surprise to me. But I was very surprised that he brought those director level supervisors into the conversation.

That is the exact type of thing that you should never do. In fact, you should work your way up the ladder one step at a time. Not jump three levels. Unfortunately for this gentleman, I'm smarter than he is.

I spent the better part of a half-hour drafting up something of a masterpiece. My response consistent of identifying his problem, identifying the solution, and identifying why I'm unable to help him. I also had injected organizational policy, and federal policy (which is the next best thing to a law), and I tactfully rammed it down his throat with a smile.

The reality is, and he told me this on the phone, that he thought I was trying to get out of doing the work. Which is exactly why he tried pulling this type of crap on me. And yet I provided the policy references that justified what I was stating, which was the icing on the cake.

That is part of the problem with people today. I've seen this personally in my own business. People are too quick to make something your fault or your problem, when in fact they just can't do the work, or they don't know how to do it. When I first started taking on clients in the web development space, I'd see this in people weekly, and at times, daily.

At no point in time should that every justify you making things personal or crossing a line that you can't come back from. This is even more important to note within email. That's because we as humans get tone from a person's voice. When you are writing an email, it's hard to get tone, which is why it normally will cut to the heart when you write something that is uncalled for.

CHAPTER 11

Final Remarks

We've covered quite a bit of tactics and options for writing up a proper email in the workplace. While it's important to note all that has been mentioned here, it's also realistic to note that not everyone will be able to effectively apply this to their work.

Everyone is different. We all process information differently, and we all perceive things differently. The reason why understanding these matters is because many people reading this likely won't process or perceive information the same as me.

While it's my hope that the world as a whole will improve on their email communication, it's also realistic to understand that nothing may change. If you are unable to follow this system, which works best for me, you shouldn't dwell on it. Instead, take what you can from this book, apply what you can, and build your own systems for email writing.

To be fully transparent, I didn't have these established systems written down anywhere before starting this book. In fact, as I was writing this, I thought about the things that I've done over the years. When doing so, I realized that I've had these systems in place for years. Which was quite profound for me, to learn that I'd built my own email communication system of methodologies without even realizing it.

Before starting to write this book, I thought that no one had ever written an email etiquette book before. And I was quite baffled that I'd never heard of it. I know now that this won't be the only book out there, and I've never read any of these other books. But I'm sure this one will be near the top.

For anyone serious about running a business, you'll definitely need to buy software and tools to help you get the job done. One of those products really needs to be the Microsoft Office suite of software, including Outlook.

No, I'm not a salesman for Microsoft. I just really, really, believe in their Office suite of products. I've been using this software since it was on Windows '95, which is about twenty-five years now. Even today, I still use Outlook, Word and Excel daily.

In fact, I use their software daily on a Windows computer and on my iMac. That's how much I use their software. For transparency, I prefer the Windows versions of the software, but that's likely because I've used Windows computers my whole life.

I know many companies, especially in the digital space where my business operates, is really big on using webmail options like

FINAL REMARKS

Google's G-Suite. In fact, for over a year on a subcontract, I used the G-Suite webmail as well.

I cannot, in good confidence, recommend any webmail option over using Outlook on your computer. In fact, I would never recommend any desktop software for email other than Outlook. It's THAT good. It's THAT powerful.

When I worked at the University of Central Arkansas, in the Reserve Officer's Training Corps (ROTC) department, we had a university email. At the time, the university had the Office 2016 suite of products, but still chose to use a severely outdated piece of email software. It blew my mind for the longest time.

Fortunately, I was able to work with the local Information Technology (IT) people and was eventually able to use Outlook instead of that old and outdated software. It was as if I'd been digging for oil my whole life and finally struck oil. I'd hope by now they've updated their software across the board, but I have no way of knowing.

I cannot stress enough that this entire book is based on my own utilization of emails, as well as, my personal obversions. These views and perspectives are in no way supported or affiliated by any of my employers. I'd like to believe that they agree with me, but I'm solely responsible for these works.

Writing an email is very similar to writing a letter. It should not be written utilizing short-hand forms of communication, such as, what would be acceptable for texting or social media. NO! This is an email, which is official correspondence of your job.

The goal is to maintain professionalism of the highest levels at all times. Removing your emotion from the equation, presenting the facts, and being direct every time. That doesn't mean that you need to lose a piece of your personality when you are writing up an email.

It does mean that your subjective and emotional nature should be mostly suppressed, and all efforts should be focused on remaining as objective as possible. Get in, deliver the facts, get out.

A letter will have an opening salutation, body and closing salutation. It will most likely have a signature as well. With email, however, we have many more options at our fingertips.

"With great power, comes great responsibility".

—Uncle Ben, Spiderman (2002)

It's because we have the power to send a "letter" in ten seconds, and it could be received in another five seconds, that we have to hone into the proper utility of this power.

We should be using the proper greeting of the day when talking to people, but also in our emails. If you did nothing more than add a good signature, and used the greeting of the day, this alone can significantly improve a person's perception of you. I know it would improve mine.

The reality is that most people don't care, and they should. When you care, you put forth more effort. When you put forth more effort, you grow and sharpen your skills. When you sharpen

FINAL REMARKS

your skills, you are naturally afforded more opportunities in life, business and your workplace.

One day, this could be the difference between your success, or your ultimate demise.

You decide.

www.ingramcontent.com/pod-product-compliance
Lightning Source LLC
Chambersburg PA
CBHW031419210526
45464CB00005B/1963